AF820369

LifeLight

"In Him was life, and the life was the light of men." John 1:4

Hosea/Joel/Amos

LEADERS GUIDE

CONCORDIA PUBLISHING HOUSE • SAINT LOUIS

The prophets Hosea, Joel, and Amos address the profound spiritual problems of Israel and Judah, calling the people to repentance while also announcing that God promised grace in the coming Savior. Oddly, in Juan de Borgoña's High Renaissance painting of Amos, he mistakenly includes a quote from Hosea: "Out of Egypt I called My son" (11:1).

Copyright © 2014 Concordia Publishing House
3558 S. Jefferson Ave., St. Louis, MO 63118-3968
1-800-325-3040 • www.cph.org

All rights reserved. No part of this publication may be reproduced, stored in a retrieval system, or transmitted, in any form or by any means, electronic, mechanical, photocopying, recording, or otherwise, without the prior written permission of Concordia Publishing House.

Written by Geoffrey R. Boyle

Edited by Brian Chisamore

Cover: *The Prophet Amos*, by Juan de Borgoña. SuperStock/SuperStock

Unless otherwise indicated, Scripture quotations are from the ESV Bible® (The Holy Bible, English Standard Version®), copyright © 2001 by Crossway Bibles, a publishing ministry of Good News Publishers. Used by permission. All rights reserved.

Scripture quotations marked NASB are taken from the New American Standard Bible®, Copyright © 1960, 1962, 1963, 1968, 1971, 1972, 1973, 1975, 1977, 1995 by The Lockman Foundation. Used by permission. (www.Lockman.org)

Scripture quotations marked KJV are from the King James or Authorized Version of the Bible.

Quotations marked *TLSB* are taken from the notes, introductory material, or original articles from *The Lutheran Study Bible* © 2009 by Concordia Publishing House. All rights reserved.

Quotations from Luther's Small Catechism are copyright © 1989 Concordia Publishing House.

The quotations from the Lutheran Confessions in this publication are from *Concordia: The Lutheran Confessions*, second edition; edited by Paul McCain, et al., copyright © 2006 Concordia Publishing House. All rights reserved. Brackets from Concordia.

Hymn texts with the abbreviation *LSB* are from *Lutheran Service Book*, copyright © 2006 Concordia Publishing House. All rights reserved.

Quotations from Luther's Works are from Martin Luther. Luther's Works. American Edition. General editors: Jaroslav Pelikan, Helmut T. Lehmann, and Christopher Boyd Brown. 75 vols. St. Louis: Concordia, and Philadelphia: Muhlenberg and Fortress, 1955– .

This publication may be available in Braille, in large print, or on cassette tape for the visually impaired. Please allow 8 to 12 weeks for delivery. Write to Lutheran Braille Workers, P.O. Box 5000, Yucaipa, CA 92399; call toll-free 1-800-925-6092; or visit the Web site: www.LBWinc.org.

Manufactured in the United States of America

1 2 3 4 5 6 7 8 9 10 23 22 21 20 19 18 17 16 15 14

Contents

Introduction

Welcome to LifeLight

A special pleasure is in store for you. You will be instrumental in leading your brothers and sisters in Christ closer to Him who is our life and light (John 1:4). You will have the pleasure of seeing fellow Christians discover new insights and rediscover old ones as they open the Scriptures and dig deep into them, perhaps deeper than they have ever dug before. More than that, you will have the pleasure of sharing in this wonderful study.

LifeLight—An In-depth Study

LifeLight is a series of in-depth Bible studies. The goal of LifeLight is that through a regular program of in-depth personal and group study of Scripture, more and more Christian adults may grow in their personal faith in Jesus Christ, enjoy fellowship with the members of His body, and reach out in love to others in witness and service.

In-depth means that this Bible study includes the following four components: individual daily home study; discussion in a small group; a lecture presentation on the Scripture portion under study; and an enhancement of the week's material (through reading the enrichment magazine).

LifeLight Participants

LifeLight participants are adults who desire a deeper study of the Scriptures than is available in the typical Sunday morning adult Bible class. (Mid-to-older teens might also be LifeLight participants.) While LifeLight does not assume an existing knowledge of the Bible or special experience or skills in Bible study, it does assume a level of commitment that will bring participants to each of the nine weekly assemblies having read the assigned readings and attempted to answer the study questions. Daily reading and study will require from 15 to 30 minutes for the five days preceding the LifeLight assembly. The day following the assembly will be spent reviewing the previous week's study by going over the completed study leaflet and the enrichment magazine.

LifeLight Leadership

While the in-depth process used by LifeLight begins with individual study and cannot achieve its aims without this individual effort, it cannot be completed by individual study alone. Therefore, trained leaders are necessary. You fill one or perhaps more of the important roles described below.

The Director

This person oversees the LifeLight program in a local center (which may be a congregation or a center operated by several neighboring congregations). The director

- serves as the parish LifeLight overall coordinator and leader;
- coordinates the scheduling of the LifeLight program;
- orders materials;
- convenes LifeLight leadership-team meetings;
- develops publicity materials;
- recruits participants;
- maintains records and budgeting;
- assigns, with the leadership team, participants to small discussion groups;
- makes arrangements for facilities;
- communicates outreach opportunities to small-group leaders and to congregational boards;
- follows up on participants who leave the program.

The Assistant Director *(optional)*

This person may assist the director. Duties listed for the director may be assigned to the assistant director as mutually agreeable.

The Lecture Leader

This person prepares and delivers the lecture at the weekly assembly. **(Lesson material for the lecture leader begins on p. 9.)** The lecture leader

- prepares and presents the Bible study lecture to the large group;

- prepares worship activities (devotional thought, hymn, prayer), using resources in the study leaflet and leaders guide and possibly other, outside sources;
- helps the small-group discussion leaders to grow in understanding the content of the lessons;
- encourages prayer at weekly leadership-team and discussion-leaders meetings.

The Small-Group Coordinator *(optional; the director may fill this role)*

This person supervises and coordinates the work of the small-group discussion leaders. The small-group coordinator

- recruits with the leadership team the small-group discussion leaders;
- trains or arranges for training of the discussion leaders;
- assists the director and discussion leaders in follow-up and outreach;
- encourages the discussion leaders to contact absent group members;
- participates in the weekly leadership-team and discussion-leaders meetings;
- provides ongoing training and support as needed.

The Small-Group Discussion Leaders

These people guide and facilitate discussion of LifeLight participants in the small groups. **(Lesson material for the small-group leaders begins on p. 57.)** There should be one discussion leader for every group of no more than twelve participants. The small-group discussion leaders are, perhaps, those individuals who are most important to the success of the program. They should, therefore, be chosen with special care and be equipped with skills needed to guide discussion and to foster a caring fellowship within the group. These discussion leaders

- prepare each week for the small-group discussion by using the study leaflet and small-group leaders guide section for that session **(see p. 57)**;
- read the enrichment magazine as a study supplement;
- guide and facilitate discussion in their small groups;
- encourage and assist the discussion groups in prayer;
- foster fellowship and mutual care within the discussion groups;
- attend weekly discussion leaders training meetings.

Leadership Training

LifeLight leaders will meet weekly to review the previous week's work and plan the coming week. At this session, leaders can address concerns and prepare for the coming session. LifeLight is a 1½-hour program with no possibility for it to be taught in the one hour typically available on Sunday mornings. Some congregations, however, may want to use the Sunday morning Bible study hour for LifeLight preparation and leadership training. In such a meeting, the lecture leader and/or small-group coordinator may lead the discussion leaders through the coming week's lesson, reserving 5 or 10 minutes for problem solving or other group concerns.

While it requires intense effort, LifeLight has proven to bring great benefit to LifeLight participants. The effort put into this program, both by leaders and by participants, will be rewarding and profitable.

The LifeLight Weekly Schedule

Here is how LifeLight will work week by week:

1. Before session 1, each participant will receive the study leaflet for session 1 and the enrichment magazine for the course. The study leaflet contains worship resources (for use both in individual daily study and at the opening of the following week's assembly) and readings and study questions for five days. Challenge questions will lead those participants who have the time and desire a greater challenge into even deeper levels of study.

2. After the five days of individual study at home, participants will gather for a weekly assembly of all LifeLight participants. The assembly will begin with a brief period of worship (5 minutes). Participants will then join their assigned small discussion groups (of twelve or fewer, who will remain the same throughout the course), where they will go over the week's study questions together (55 minutes). Assembling together once again, participants will listen to a lecture presentation on the readings they have studied in the previous week and discussed in their small groups (20 minutes). After the lecture presentation, the director or another leader will distribute the study leaflet for the following week. Closing announcements and other necessary business may take another five minutes before dismissal.

In some places some small groups will not join the weekly assembly because of scheduling or other reasons. Such groups may meet at another time and place (perhaps in the home of one of the small group's members). Those congregations may record the lecture given by the lecture leader at the weekly assembly and duplicate it for use by other groups meeting later in the week.

3. On the day following the assembly, participants will review the preceding week's work by rereading the study leaflet they completed (and that they perhaps supplemented or corrected during the discussion in their small group) and by reading appropriate articles in the enrichment magazine.

Then the LifeLight weekly study process will begin all over again!

Recommended Study Resources and Worship

The Lutheran Study Bible. St. Louis: Concordia Publishing House, 2009. This resource contains more than 26,000 study and application notes, a most thorough reference guide (pp. lxv–cx), and over 90,000 cross-references, as well as a 31,000-entry concordance, maps, charts, and timelines.

Roehrs, Walter R., and Martin H. Franzmann. *Concordia Self-Study Commentary.* St. Louis: Concordia Publishing House, 1979. This one-volume commentary on the Bible contains 950 pages and is tailored for lay use.

The Concordia Organist is a 31-CD collection of pipe organ accompaniments for all the hymns and liturgical music in *Lutheran Service Book*. St. Louis: Concordia Publishing House (order no. 99-2264). Use these CDs for worship hymn accompaniment.

Getting into the Book of the Twelve

A Survey of the Minor Prophets

Preparing for the Session

Central Focus

The "Minor Prophets" have nothing minor to deliver. What you get in this Book of the Twelve is Christ and Him crucified for Israel, for Judah, and *for you*!

Objectives

That participants, led by the Holy Spirit working through God's Word, will

1. understand the unique way in which God's Word unfolds by reading the Minor Prophets as one Book of the Twelve;
2. compare the underlying theme of this Book of the Twelve with the theme of Scripture as a whole, as seen on the cross of Christ;
3. find comfort in the sweet Gospel proclamation of the twelve prophets, receiving a new and confident hope in Christ; and
4. apply the Scripture to their own lives, growing in service to the Lord.

Note for the small-group leaders: Lesson notes and other materials you will need begin on page 55.

For the Lecture Leader

Session Plan

Worship

Begin the session with the hymn printed in the study leaflet. Accompaniments are available in denominational hymnals, such as *Lutheran Service Book* or *Lutheran Worship* (refer to hymnal index). (Note: Concordia Publishing House has available *The Concordia Organist*. All the initial worship hymns in the LifeLight courses are included in this resource. It's especially helpful for mission congregations and small parishes. See the list of study resources on page 7.) Follow with this prayer:

Prayer

O God of the prophets, as You spoke to Your people of old by the mouths of the prophets, speak again through their books and open our ears to hear. May the messages of the twelve Minor Prophets revive, for they comforted the people of Jacob and delivered them with confident hope. Give to us such a hope in Your Son, Jesus, who is the fulfillment of their words and the substance of which they preached. In the name of Jesus we pray. Amen.

Lecture Presentation

1 Introduction: One Book or Twelve?

Twelve books: each has a different name at the top of the page; each rests within a unique context; each has its own date, time, setting, and place. Twelve books—so what do we mean by "the Book of the Twelve"? Is it one, or are there twelve? And does it really matter?

Interestingly, the twelve Minor Prophets, as they've come to be known, have long been considered twelve books within one book. Just about two centuries after the writing of Malachi (the last of the Twelve), the Jewish teacher Jesus son of Sirach wrote:

> May the bones of the twelve prophets revive from where they lie,
> for they comforted the people of Jacob and delivered them with confident hope.
> (Ecclesiasticus 49:10).

This summary follows upon a summary of Isaiah, Jeremiah, and Ezekiel. It's as if the author is walking his students through the Old Testament Scriptures one by one. These Twelve Prophets are summarized by their words of "comfort" and "confident hope."

This evidence from the Apocrypha shows that early in the history of Israel, these twelve were read together as *one*. They had one message, one witness, but many voices. If we compare this Book of the Twelve with other Major Prophets—Isaiah, Jeremiah, and Ezekiel—we find that these twelve books together are roughly the same size as one of the other larger prophets.

In the decades following the destruction of the temple in AD 70, two more pieces of evidence emerge that these twelve were read together: 2 Esdras 14:45 (another apocrypha text) and the first-century writer Josephus (*Against Apion* 1:38–42). In counting the Old Testament books, both assume that the twelve count as one. This listing of books was used among the early Christians, as well as by the rabbis. The first-century Bishop Melito of Sardis says it plainly: "The twelve in one book" (Eusebius, *Ecclesiastical History*, iv.26.14). In fact, the New Testament also gives a hint of this in the Book of Acts. Luke presents a quote from Amos, saying, "As it is written in *the book* of the prophets" (Acts 7:42, emphasis added). One book, multiple prophets, and a quote from Amos: here's New Testament evidence that these twelve were read together as one. All of this goes to show the long history and tradition within both the synagogues and the churches of reading and studying these twelve prophets as one book of sacred Scripture—the Book of the Twelve.

2 Does It Matter?

So, what's the point? Does this change our reading or affect our understanding? Well, yes, and this is the point: by reading the twelve prophets as the Book of the Twelve, we will come across themes and clues, questions and answers that might not be readily available in one particular prophet but that appear in the next. Sometimes there are cliff-hangers. Sometimes the text raises a question for which we won't find a good answer until we get to the next prophet. Hosea, for instance, exhorts, (14:1) "Return, O Israel, to the Lord your God." Here is a call to repent, to come back, and the book ends with an admonition to the wise: (14:9)

> Whoever is wise, let him understand these things;
> whoever is discerning, let him know them;
> for the ways of the Lord are right,
> and the upright walk in them,
> but transgressors stumble in them.

So does Israel return and walk in the Lord's ways—understanding and discerning what is right? Hosea doesn't tell us! He just ends his book. But, as soon as you flip the page and pick up Joel, you find not only the continued theme of returning but also that the answer is "No!" And so Joel again issues the call: (2:12) "Return to Me with all your heart."

Or take Jonah: when he finally gets to Nineveh, proclaims the Lord's call to repentance (returning), and then sits back waiting for the city to be destroyed, he realizes that our Lord has had mercy on Nineveh. The Lord heard their cry, saw their repentance, and saved them (Jonah 3:10). But just two books later, in Nahum, we see that this mighty Nineveh has again turned from the Lord. You see, within these twelve books of prophecy we have many connections, many ties from one to the next, from first to last, and all sorts in between. Reading the Twelve as one book allows us to ask questions not only of what Hosea meant in a certain isolated context but also of what Hosea has to say in light of Malachi and the rest of the Twelve. This sort of reading invites a look to the beginning and the end. It invites us to see various themes, rhythms, and cycles, and to cling to certain words intentionally repeated and emphasized.

3 The Day of the Lord

So what are some of these themes? For starters, a major unifying theme throughout the Book of the Twelve is "the day of the Lord." This *day* is a day of both judgment and restoration. It is a day of great pain and recompense, but also a day of salvation and new life. Hosea introduces this day, saying, (1:11) "great shall be the day of Jezreel." For Hosea, that day is a day of great reversal: judgment turns to blessing, mercy comes where there is "No Mercy," and, (Hosea 2:16, 18, 20) "In that day, declares the Lord, you will call Me 'My Husband,' and no longer will you call Me 'My Baal.' . . . And I will make for them a covenant on that day. . . . And you shall know the Lord." Joel shows this day to be a day of great destruction: (1:15) "Alas for the day! For the day of the Lord is near, and as destruction from the Almighty it comes"; (2:1–2) "The day of the Lord is coming; it is near, a day of darkness and gloom, a day of clouds and thick darkness!" Amos recognizes some misunderstanding about whether the day is a good thing or bad: (5:18) "Woe to you who desire the day of the Lord! Why would you have the day of the Lord? It is darkness, and not light." Obadiah, who preaches a strong message of repentance to the Gentiles, also warns: (v. 15) "For the day of the Lord is near upon all the nations."

We get the sense at the end of Obadiah that there is no hope for the Gentiles, for those nations outside of Israel. But then comes Jonah, giving a resounding "YES!" to the nations—even Nineveh! For Jonah, the Day of the Lord is not mentioned because, for Nineveh (at least for now), the Day of the Lord has not come.

Micah speaks of the healing and miracles that will come: (4:6–7) "In that day, declares the Lord, I will assemble the lame and gather those who have been driven away and those whom I have afflicted; and the lame I will make the remnant, and those who were cast off, a strong nation." Nahum sees "the chariots come with flashing metal on the day He [the Lord] musters them" (2:3); Habakkuk "will quietly wait for the day of trouble" (3:16); and Zephaniah calls all to "be silent before the Lord God! For the day of the Lord is near" (1:7). Then Zephaniah launches into a litany of what that day will be like: (vv. 14–16, 18)

> The great day of the Lord is near,
> near and hastening fast;
> the sound of the day of the Lord is bitter;
> the mighty man cries aloud there.
> A day of wrath is that day,
> a day of distress and anguish,
> a day of ruin and devastation,
> a day of darkness and gloom,
> a day of clouds and thick darkness,
> a day of trumpet blast and battle cry
> against the fortified cities
> and against the lofty battlements.
> Neither their silver nor their gold
> shall be able to deliver them
> on the day of the wrath of the Lord.

In fact, this text of Zephaniah inspired the thirteenth-century Latin hymn *Dies Irae*, which we sing today as the hymn "Day of Wrath, O Day of Mourning" (*The Lutheran Hymnal* 607). This hymn (all nineteen stanzas!) rightly locates this Day of the Lord as ultimately fulfilled on the cross: (stanza 19)

> To the rest Thou didst prepare me
> On Thy cross; O Christ, upbear me!
> Spare, O God, in mercy spare me!

The last portion of the Book of the Twelve again sees this day as a day of promise for Israel. Haggai proclaims: (2:23) "On that day, declares the Lord of hosts, I will take you, O Zerubbabel My servant, the son of Shealtiel, declares the Lord, and make you like a signet ring, for I have chosen you, declares the Lord of hosts." Zechariah likewise heralds great promises of joy for Israel: (9:16) "On that day the Lord their God will save them, as the flock of His people; for like the jewels of a crown they shall shine on His land." Like Zephaniah, Zechariah also provides a litany of events for that day, all confessing the salvation of the people. For example, in Zechariah 12–14, nearly every other verse begins with the words "On that day." In fact, the very last words of Zechariah are "on that day" (14:21).

Finally, near the end of the Book of the Twelve, Malachi asks, (3:2) "But who can endure the day of His coming, and who can stand when He appears?" So there's no confusion, he answers it for us: (4:1–3)

> For behold, the day is coming, burning like an oven, when all the arrogant and all evildoers will be stubble. The day that is coming shall set them ablaze, says the Lord of hosts, so that it will leave them neither root nor branch. But for you who fear My name, the sun of righteousness shall rise with healing in its wings. You shall go out leaping like calves from the stall. And you shall tread down the wicked, for they will be ashes under the soles of your feet, on the day when I act, says the Lord of hosts.

Before that day comes, Malachi also promises, will be the coming of Elijah (Malachi 4:5). He will turn us through repentance and stretch out his bony finger, proclaiming: (John 1:29) "Behold, the Lamb of God, who takes away the sin of the world!" Jesus says of John the Baptizer, (Matthew 11:14) "he is Elijah who is to come."

As we see, this the Day of the Lord runs consistently throughout the twelve Minor Prophets. This theme helps us to understand the purpose of the Twelve. It guides our reading, tunes our ears to what our Lord wants to say to us, and ultimately thrusts us forward into the New Testament, where we see the Day of the Lord finally fulfilled: on the cross of Christ. Understanding this fulfillment is the key to our reading not only of this Book of the Twelve but also, in fact, the entire Old Testament.

4 On the Timeline

But don't these twelve prophets cover many years and multiple locations? Yes, they do! That appears to be roughly how they are organized. Half of these prophetic books tell us exactly when the prophet preached; the other half don't—at least, not explicitly. The Books of Hosea, Amos, Micah, Zephaniah, Haggai, and Zechariah all begin with something like: "The word of the Lord that came to *X*, the son of *X*, in the days of *X*."

This is called a superscription. This sort of thing appears in each of the Major Prophets as well. Superscriptions tell us when the prophet received the Word of the Lord; and it's normally marked by which king is ruling at the time. So Hosea and Amos are contemporaries, because the kings who reigned in their days were roughly the same. Amos 1:1 lists only Uzziah of Judah and Jeroboam of Israel, but Hosea 1:1 gives the fuller length of his preaching: "Uzziah, Jotham, Ahaz, and Hezekiah, kings of Judah, and in the days of Jeroboam the son of Joash, king of Israel." Whether Amos's ministry was shorter than Hosea's, we don't know. What we do know is that they are the earliest of the Twelve that we can date, and Micah isn't far behind (he begins in the days of Jotham, just missing Uzziah; see Micah 1:1). This sets at least Hosea and Amos in the middle of the eighth century BC, covering roughly from 753 to 715 BC. Isaiah and Micah aren't far behind.

Zephaniah receives the word of the Lord (1:1) "in the days of Josiah the son of Amon, king of Judah." King Josiah began his reign in 640 BC in Jerusalem as a young eight-year-old boy, and served until his untimely death at the battle of Megiddo in 609 BC (2 Kings 22:1; 23:29). Sometime during this reign, Zephaniah served Israel as prophet, placing him just before Jeremiah, whose prophecy begins roughly at the end of Josiah's reign.

Haggai and Zechariah are the last two who tell us when their prophecy occurred—indeed, they're also the most exact! Haggai says, (1:1) "In the second year of Darius the king, in the sixth month, on the first day of the month, the word of the Lord came by the hand of Haggai the prophet to Zerubbabel." This locates us somewhere between August and September of 520 BC. Martin Luther rightly shows that "Haggai is the first prophet given to the people after the Babylonian captivity" (AE 35:329). With Haggai is Zechariah; the two overlap quite a bit. Zechariah begins: (1:1) "In the eighth month, in the second year of Darius, the word of the Lord came to the prophet Zechariah, the son of Berechiah, son of Iddo." This puts Zechariah's first prophecy about two months after Haggai's. The two are one prophetic voice that accompanies the rededication of the temple as built under the leadership of Ezra and Nehemiah.

So, from the six superscriptions, we understand this Book of the Twelve spans from roughly 753 to 515 BC—and this doesn't even address the other six books that do not provide dates for their writing. Joel's prophecy suggests it might be located somewhere in the ninth century BC (e.g., Joel 3:2 mentions Jehoshaphat, who reigned 873–848 BC), which would make his prophecy the earliest written work, but this is questionable (see Joel 3:6, which mentions the Greeks). On the other hand, Malachi likely dates somewhere around the middle of the fifth century BC, making his the last of the written prophecies. With multiple centuries, with some prophets addressing Israel in the north and others addressing Judah in the south—what unity can there be?

5 The Ultimate Point

This brings us to the higher purpose of the Twelve: to proclaim Jesus Christ and Him crucified (1 Corinthians 2:2). He is the purpose of *all* the prophets. He is their vision. He is their revelation. He is the Word that came to them. All prophecy is finally a forth-telling of Christ. It's the proclamation of God's will for man, and this Bible study will show how this is so. And what is God's will? (Luke 24:46–47) "That the Christ should suffer and on the third day rise from the dead, and that repentance and forgiveness of sins should be proclaimed in His name to all nations." The apostles witnessed these very events. The prophets foretold them. They saw and heard of them as the Word of the Lord came to them; but they saw as through a veil—the full meaning was hidden from them for a time. And so they proclaimed this Christ through poetry, through parable, and through visions of destruction but also of promise. The ultimate purpose of these twelve holy prophets is to call sinners to repentance and to hold before their eyes the salvation that God Himself would deliver. They proclaim the Day of the Lord. They proclaim His righteous judgment and His merciful redemption. They proclaim the Lord's killing and His making alive. For these twelve, it's always Christ, God Himself, who is coming for us and for our salvation.

It is in Christ that God will "restore the fortunes of My people Israel" (Amos 9:14). It's in Christ that "the exiles of this host of the people of Israel shall possess the land . . . and the kingdom shall be the Lord's" (Obadiah 20–21). It's in Christ that the Gentiles will be saved (think Nineveh!) and that from Bethlehem, "too little to be among the clans of Judah, . . . shall come forth for Me one who is to be ruler in Israel" (Micah 5:2). And it is in Christ that the daughter of Zion will sing and shout aloud and Israel will rejoice (Zephaniah 3:14; Zechariah 9:9). For Jesus Christ alone will suffer the rejection and death that all prophets point toward: (Zechariah 12:10) "When they look on Me, on Him whom they have pierced"; (Zechariah 13:7) "Strike the shepherd, and the sheep will be scattered." "But," Malachi 4:2 reminds us, "for you who fear My name, the sun of righteousness shall rise with healing in its wings. You shall go out leaping like calves from the stall."

That is the point of the Twelve: Jesus Christ is the One who suffers, dies, and rises *for you!* Repent and be glad! Shout aloud and sing for joy! For you a Savior has gone up Mount Zion, and the kingdom is the Lord's!

Conclusion: Getting It Law/Gospel Right!

Now, this Christ that each of the twelve prophets saw under the revelation of visions certainly comes to us in two ways. That's how all of Scripture comes: by way of Law and Gospel, judgment and forgiveness, cursing and blessing. Looking again at one of the foundational themes of this Book of the Twelve, Dr. Reed Lessing gets it right:

> When "the Day of [the Lord]" texts from the Twelve are placed together, the two themes of Law and Gospel emerge: it will be a day of destruction for the ungodly but also a day of salvation for the righteous. Usually it is described as a day of judgment, but it can also be the decisive time of grace. (*Amos* [St. Louis: CPH, 2009], 14–15)

This is true, not only for this day, but also for this Christ they proclaim. The cross itself is both joy and sadness, life and death, judgment and blessing. For those who reject Christ, the cross is simply another foolish act, along with healing the sick, exorcising the demons, and raising the dead. But for those of us who confess our sins, who admit to our own guilt and shame, who see ourselves in the shoes of Gomer or Nineveh, that cross is a life-giving tree.

Getting Law and Gospel straight will do wonders at making sense of this Book of the Twelve. We must not shy away from its strict words of judgment, understanding that all judgment is ultimately poured out upon Christ on the cross. Nor can we minimize the great and expansive words of redemption, for those are ours in Christ!

In each unique context, the twelve Minor Prophets consistently preach Christ. Whether it's the false worship Amos addresses at Bethel and Gilgal in the eighth century BC or the rise of Babylonian power with Zephaniah in the seventh century BC or the return to Jerusalem in the Persian period of the late sixth century BC—in all contexts and all times and all places, the coming of Christ is proclaimed as a word of comfort to distressed and guilty consciences, as well as a word of rebuke and admonition to those comfortable in their sin. In all twelve, salvation and redemption is always God's work done in the promised Christ. Punishment and destruction are always on account of man's disobedience and willful, unrepentant sin.

While many might read this Book of the Twelve and think it rather Law-heavy, consider again the summary from Jesus son of Sirach:

> May the bones of the twelve prophets revive
> from where they lie,
> for they comforted the people of Jacob and
> delivered them with confident hope.
> (Ecclesiasticus 49:10).

May the meditation on God's Word from these first three books of the twelve Minor Prophets—Hosea, Joel, and Amos—revive and comfort you through their proclamation of the Gospel of Christ.

Concluding Activities

Conclude the session with an appropriate prayer and distribute the study leaflet for week 2.

A Mysterious Love Story

Hosea 1–3

Preparing for the Session

Central Focus

Hosea sets the stage for the Book of the Twelve to be a story of repentance and great reversals, where God ultimately wins us back with His unquenchable and gracious love for us.

Objectives

That participants, led by the Holy Spirit working through God's Word, will

1. recognize that the relationship between Hosea and Gomer is a depiction of God's love for us;
2. interpret the great reversals of Hosea in light of the great reversal that Christ enacts on the cross for us; and
3. come to critique their own lives in terms of repentance and absolution, recognizing the depths to which God descends for them in Christ.

Note for the small-group leaders: Lesson notes and other materials you will need begin on page 58.

For the Lecture Leader

Session Plan

Worship

Begin the session with the hymn printed in the study leaflet. Accompaniments are available in denominational hymnals, such as *Lutheran Service Book* or *Lutheran Worship* (refer to hymnal index). (Note: Concordia Publishing House has available *The Concordia Organist*. All the initial worship hymns in the LifeLight courses are included in this resource. It's especially helpful for mission congregations and small parishes. See the list of study resources on page 7.) Follow with this prayer:

Prayer

O Blessed Christ, You give what is Yours and take what is ours. You bless us with this happy exchange. As You have united Yourself to us in the wedding feast of Your Sacrament, create within us thankful hearts to recognize that You have given us everything by Your grace alone. For You live and reign with the Father and the Holy Spirit, in blessed communion, now and forever. Amen.

Lecture Presentation

1 Gomer: An Unlikely Wife

Our reason rebels against the very notion! God wouldn't do that—would He? A harlot? A prostitute? A "wife of whoredom" (Hosea 1:2)? No, not our Lord; not His prophet.

And yet, the plain sense of the book tells us God really did set up His prophet with such a woman. Not only was she unclean when Hosea took her, but everyone knew she had a propensity to return to that uncleanness!

Gomer, "daughter of Diblaim" (1:3), was probably not yet a prostitute when Hosea was first took her as his wife. She was probably a young girl who had not remained chaste. Though not so shocking in today's culture, it was a horrible offense in ancient Israel. She lost her virginity before marriage. And while such a discovery might legally have resulted in her stoning (as required in Deuteronomy 22:20–21), this is the first grace given to Gomer—she lives! God commands His prophet to take an unchaste woman for his wife, and it is with her he is to have children and establish a family. It seems surprising of our Lord, who commands chastity in the Sixth Commandment and also repeatedly commands stoning for those who break it (Leviticus 20:10; John 8:5).

So Hosea takes this unworthy Gomer as his wife. In chapter 1, we see that Gomer bears Hosea three children: two sons and a daughter. Assuming a normal course of pregnancy and standard weaning (by age 2 or 3), it seems that Gomer and Hosea were together for at least six or seven years.

And then something happens. Chapter 2 shifts our focus: first, because the chapter is largely poetry, not the prose we saw in chapter 1; and second, because this chapter wavers back and forth between describing typical prophecy and the marriage of Hosea and Gomer. This ambiguity between the themes is intentional. After reading chapter 2, we wonder, "Was that about Hosea and Gomer, or God and His people?"—which is the prophet's goal.

Here, Hosea addresses his children and begs of them, (2:2) "Plead with your mother, plead." He then speaks of the reality of their divorce because of her unfaithfulness. Hosea pleads with his children to call their mother to account, to stop her adultery. Verse 3 is one of those ambiguous passages: is this the Lord speaking, or Hosea, or both?

> Lest I strip her naked
> and make her as in the day she was born,
> and make her like a wilderness,
> and make her like a parched land,
> and kill her with thirst.

The imagery of this verse compares well with the picture of Judah's unfaithfulness that Ezekiel presents:

> (16:3–5) Thus says the Lord God to Jerusalem: Your origin and your birth are of the land of the Canaanites; your father was an Amorite and your mother a Hittite. And as for your birth, on the day you were born your cord was not cut, nor were you washed with water to cleanse you, nor rubbed with salt, nor wrapped in swaddling cloths. No eye pitied you, to do any of these things to you out of compassion for you, but you were cast out on the open field, for you were abhorred, on the day that you were born.

Gomer is the image of sinful Israel: unclean from birth, adulterous, and full of unquenchable lust for other lovers. In fact, it is difficult to find much about Gomer that is not also and primarily about Israel, about us.

But notice that even when she is in the midst of her adultery—even caught in the act, much like the woman of John 8:1–11—our Lord comes in mercy: (Hosea 2:14, 16, 20)

> Therefore, behold, I will allure her, and bring her into the wilderness, and speak tenderly to her. . . . In that day, declares the Lord, you will call Me "My Husband." . . . I will betroth you to Me in faithfulness.

Gomer will be sought after, despite her sin. She will be pursued and chased and run after, just as in Jesus' parable when the father runs to his prodigal son (Luke 15:20). The more we learn about Gomer, the more we learn of the depths of our Lord's mercy for us and for all His people.

Chapter 3 draws us back into the story of Hosea. We return to prose, not poetry. Here we see the Lord commanding Hosea: (v. 1) "Go again, love a woman who is loved by another man and is an adulteress." For the record, this isn't another woman; it's Gomer again. Hosea is to take her back, love her again. But there's a twist. Not only has she been adulterous but it is also quite likely that her adultery has landed her in a prostitution ring. That's what it means when Hosea says, (v. 3) "So I bought her for fifteen shekels of silver and a homer and a lethech of barley." The price was comparable to buying a slave, freeing her from her bondage to life as a prostitute. Hosea, who had already married her, now buys his wife back—this is the second grace. He again vows his faithfulness and demands the same of her (v. 3). And that's the last we hear of Gomer.

No one would consider Gomer a good spouse. She was undesirable, unchaste, prone to whoredom, caught in adultery, sold into prostitution, and almost worthless. Nothing good is spoken about her, not one thing to her credit. She has only Hosea's love. And as we see this marriage and family unfolding before our eyes as an image of Christ and His Church, we rejoice in knowing that what goes for Gomer goes also for us. We also have nothing: (Romans 3:12) "all have turned aside; together [we] have become worthless." All we have is Christ's tireless love. That is the point of this book of prophecy: salvation is utterly up to God and depends solely on His love, His faithfulness toward us. He loves us, joins His life to ours, calls us His own, and brings us back again from our wandering ways. He buys us back, "not with gold or silver, but with His holy, precious blood and with His innocent suffering and death" (Small Catechism, Second Article). Like Gomer, we are the unworthy, unexpected spouse of God Himself in Christ.

2 The Children: Named for Reversal

As for the children, each is given a name you won't find on any baby-name list: Jezreel (the location of a bloody coup), Lo-ruhama (meaning "No Mercy"), and Lo-ammi (meaning "Not My People"). Each is named in the way of judgment.

> (1:4) Call his name Jezreel, for in just a little while I will punish the house of Jehu for the blood of Jezreel.

> (1:6) Call her name No Mercy, for I will no more have mercy on the house of Israel, to forgive them at all.

> (1:9) Call his name Not My People, for you are not My people, and I am not your God.

While the children are named for judgment, we are also told early on of their great reversal: (1:10–11)

> Yet the number of the children of Israel shall be like the sand of the sea, which cannot be measured or numbered. And in the place where it was said to them, "You are not My people," it shall be said to them, "Children of the living God." . . . And they shall go up from the land, for great shall be the day of Jezreel.

Now, it is easy to understand the reversal of the second two children; Hosea says, (2:23) "And I will have mercy on No Mercy, and I will say to Not My People, 'You are My people.'"

We know the Lord cannot go long without having mercy. That's simply who He is. When Moses asked to see God's glory, the Lord hid Moses in the cleft of a rock. Passing by, He revealed to Moses His name: (Exodus 34:6) "The Lord, the Lord, a God merciful and gracious, slow to anger, and abounding in steadfast love and faithfulness." God's self-confession repeats itself throughout the Book of the Twelve. If there's something to know about the God of Israel, it is precisely this: He is the God of mercy.

The same goes for the youngest child, Not My People. To be the people of God is to be chosen and brought into a covenant with the Lord. Israel broke the covenant. They wanted a Lord other than this God of mercy. To have another Lord is then to be another people; so the judgment: "Not My People." Yet the day of great reversal, the Day of the Lord, will again reinstate the covenant between the Lord and His people Israel. They again will be brought into His kingdom "and serve Him in everlasting righteousness, innocence, and blessedness" (Small Catechism, Second Article).

We also see the fulfillment of the names of these last two children in the New Testament: (1 Peter 2:10) "Once you were not a people, but now you are God's people; once you had not received mercy, but now you have received mercy." Here, Peter shows how we Gentiles are prefigured in the younger children of the prophet Hosea. But what about the eldest? What of Jezreel?

The name Jezreel has both positive and negative connotations in itself, which is why, when the day of great reversals comes (Hosea 1:10–11; 2:22–23), his name doesn't change like the others. The name Jezreel first appears in Joshua 15:56 as one of the cities listed in Judah's inheritance of the land. Though many important political figures come from Jezreel, what gives meaning to its usage here is to the blood that was shed when the prophet Elisha sent one of the "sons of the prophets" (see *TLSB*, p. 555) to anoint Jehu as king of Israel (2 Kings 9:1–13). Once Jehu is heralded as king of Israel, the massacre begins. Jehu's revolution concludes: (10:11) "so Jehu struck down all who remained of the house of Ahab in Jezreel, all his great men and his close friends and his priests, until he left him none remaining."

All of this takes place in Jezreel. Blood, judgment—it all comes to mind with the birth and naming of Hosea's first child. That's his judgment—or better yet, Israel's judgment lived out prophetically by Hosea's eldest son.

But what about the reversal? How does this Valley of Judgment and Blood turn into a blessing, as the other children do? What does Hosea mean (1:11) "great shall be the day of Jezreel"? Or when he says, (2:21–23a) "'And in that day I will answer, declares the Lord, I will answer the heavens, and they shall answer the earth, and the earth shall answer the grain, the wine, and the oil, and they shall answer Jezreel, and I will sow her for Myself in the land"?

Notice the agricultural language: rain speaks to land, and land to grain, wine, and oil. These then answer Jezreel. Jezreel is Hebrew for "God sows." The Valley of Jezreel was known for its fertility. The area is a fault basin, receiving an abundance of water. The day of great reversals brings for Jezreel a reinstatement of what his name intends for him to be: sown by God.

So each child—Jezreel, No Mercy, and Not My People—is named for judgment and cursing. Then, on the day of great reversals, each is turned from judgment to mercy, curse to blessing, death to life. As it was for the children of Hosea, so also for the Israelites of old as they repented of their idolatry and clung again to their merciful God of the covenant. And as it was for the Israelites of old, so it is also for us! In Christ, all the judgments and all the curses find their end. The blood that was shed on Mount Calvary sunk much deeper and more profoundly into the land than the centuries of blood in the Valley of Jezreel. The fruit that sprang from the Valley of Jezreel was only a foretaste of the fruit that was to spring from Mount Zion—from the cross, we all receive the fruit of redemption: the forgiveness of sins and life everlasting.

3 Hosea: Living the Prophetic Word

So what about Hosea and his family? The first three chapters of Hosea are a classic example of what is called a "prophetic sign-act." That is, while typical prophecy pertains solely to the speaking of words, a sign-act requires also a *sign*, an event. It is a history-creating expression of the Divine Word that is tangible: visible, touchable, smellable and, if you like, even tasteable. So with Hosea, his wife, and his three children, we not only have preaching but we also have the sign of their lives and deeds as a living prophecy. Some have called these prophecies *word events*. Perhaps more liturgically, we would call them *sacramentals*, forerunners of what we find in the Sacraments (Word and element).

Such prophetic sign-acts are common in the Old Testament. For example, Ezekiel lay on his left side for 390 days, bearing the punishment of the house of Israel (Ezekiel 4:4–5). Jeremiah wore a heavy yoke around his neck as a warning for those who would not submit to Nebuchadnezzar and the Babylonians (Jeremiah 27:1–7). Isaiah strolled about naked and barefoot for three years as a sign against Egypt and Cush (Isaiah 20:1–4). These are just a few of the examples that pepper the Scriptures. But what does this tell us about Hosea? Or better yet, what does Hosea (and his family) tell us about our Lord?

Hosea's personal life and prophetic office were intertwined. He did not get to "clock out" when he went home. He was never off duty. That's the life of a prophet. So Hosea is a suffering prophet. While men of valor can surely endure great pains for the sake of others, whenever the family is brought into the suffering, everything changes. Hosea's family was not only open to the public eye but his wife and children were in fact part of the prophecy itself! Their lives were living testimonies of what our Lord would do with His people. This tells us much of the character of our Lord: He calls the whole person into service. Our Lord entrusted His prophet with the Word. This Word, which could be found only in the voice of the prophet, also attached itself to the person of the prophet (and here, even his family). All of this prepares us well to see in Christ the fulfillment of the prophets, where the Word becomes flesh and dwells among us. It also helps to make sense of Hosea. The first three chapters are largely this prophetic sign-act. Chapters 4 through 14 will be the preaching that accompanies this strange marriage and family.

We should be clear, however, that sign-acts are not mere allegories or symbols. Real life bears a real message. Hosea really married Gomer. They really had children. Those children really had those awful names of judgment. But what does it all mean? Well, that's what the book unfolds for us along the way. But right up front, we know that this is all a prophecy of God's relation to His people Israel. Hosea is an image of God (most clearly, God in Christ). Gomer represents sinful Israel. She was filthy when Hosea found her, just as Israel was wallowing in her own sinfulness. The children all represent the people of Israel, the sons and daughters of Israel. Adultery is the consistent image of Israel's idolatry. The initial marriage represents the initial covenant; the remarriage is the reestablished covenant—the new covenant that Christ tells us is in His blood (Luke 22:20).

The parallels go on and on, and that is where the theology is richest! Chapter 2 shows the fine line between the prophecy and the sign-act. When Hosea says, (v. 14) "Therefore, behold, I will allure her, and bring her into the wilderness, and speak tenderly to her," is this his wooing of Gomer, or the Lord's wooing of us in Christ? Perhaps it would be best to say both!

4 Happy Exchange

The historical context of Hosea's marriage is difficult to pinpoint. We know Hosea carried out his prophetic ministry roughly sometime between 753 and 735 BC. His message is addressed to the Northern Kingdom of Israel, though Judah in the south listens in along the way. Beyond that general background, we can't get much closer. Hosea is tantalizingly obscure when it comes to political figures. Though frustrating for the historian, this permits and encourages the hearer of every time and place to hear this Word of prophecy as a Word that extends beyond eighth-century Israel. Each of us is intended to perceive in Hosea's marriage a divine message of mercy and great reversals that is also for us!

These great reversals—or as Luther famously called them, "happy exchanges"—come with a clear call to repentance. As we know, repentance has two parts: confessing our sins and then receiving forgiveness. The confession of sins comes about only after an awareness of sin: the preaching of the Law. The sin Israel is abundantly guilty of is idolatry. Within the marriage metaphor, that's what all this talk of adultery is about: (Hosea 2:5b) "For she said, 'I will go after my lovers.'" The manifestation of her adultery is idolatry, the false worship of false gods—most notably, Baal: (2:13) "And I will punish her for the feast days of the Baals . . . her lovers." This is the Law Hosea presents before the people of Israel: the god(s) you worship are not the one, true God. Israel's worship and prayers have faltered from the fear, love, and trust in the Lord, the God of Israel. As we enter the main body of Hosea's prophecy, we'll find many more details of this false worship. For now, it's enough to know that both Israel's doctrine of God and Israel's worship have together gone far astray—so much so that God must act. He acts first in the preaching (and living) of this word of judgment against Israel—hence the names Not My People and No Mercy. This is the first part of repentance: recognizing and admitting guilt. The second part is to receive absolution, forgiveness. And this comes also from the Lord: (2:14) "Therefore, behold, I will allure her, and bring her into the wilderness, and speak tenderly to her." This is the gentle word of sins forgiven. That's our Lord's wooing of Israel, of us. Notably, it all takes place in that day.

We've already discussed at length the importance of the Day of the Lord for the Book of the Twelve. For Hosea, it is the day when Israel is forgiven, loved again by the Lord. This is prophesied in Hosea's own life, as he, in chapter 3, buys Gomer back and restores her to his household. This Day of the Lord is the day of great reversals, of happy exchanges—the day when the broken covenant is restored and (3:5) "the children of Israel shall return and seek the Lord their God, and David their king, and they shall come in fear to the Lord and to His goodness in the latter days."

Conclusion: The Mystery of Christ and His Church

Hosea's family carries his prophetic message in tangible ways. They live his prophecy. So, when Hosea pleads to Gomer to repent, to turn from her ways (Hosea 2:2), our Lord pleads with His people Israel to repent; and along with them, with us as well. This marriage is a mystery. While we may glean some dos and don'ts for marriage counseling, that is not the intention. The purpose of all marriage sign-acts, metaphors, and imagery throughout the Scriptures is to proclaim Jesus Christ. He is the faithful groom who saw Israel wallowing in her blood (Ezekiel 16). He is the faithful groom that bought Gomer back from prostitution. Paul says, (Ephesians 5:32) "This mystery is profound, and I am saying that it refers to Christ and the church." The mystery of marriage is that it presents before us an image of Christ's love toward us, His Church.

What makes this mystery so glorious is the happy exchange: we get the Lord, and He gets us. Gomer receives the honor of Hosea, while Hosea takes on the adultery of Gomer. Her iniquity becomes his; his righteousness hers. That's Jesus for you. He gets into the filthy baptismal waters; whatever flowed off you gathers right onto Him. It's a mystery; it's the Gospel; it's the message of Hosea 1–3.

Concluding Activities

Conclude the session with an appropriate prayer and distribute the study leaflet for week 3.

Standing Trial

Hosea 4:1–11:11

Preparing for the Session

Central Focus

The God who acts does so in terms of Law and Gospel. He brings us up on charges that we are all guilty of; and then, by the judgment rendered on His Son, sets us free. This we must learn to know over and over and over again!

Objectives

That participants, led by the Holy Spirit working through God's Word, will

1. understand who they are in light of Israel's sins of old;
2. recognize who God is—the One who brings repentance and new life;
3. distinguish between these two understandings, trusting God to do all things well for them; and
4. daily repent from sins of omission and commission, and live actively by faith.

Note for the small-group leaders: Lesson notes and other materials you will need begin on page 60.

For the Lecture Leader

Session Plan

Worship

Begin the session with the hymn printed in the study leaflet. Accompaniments are available in denominational hymnals, such as *Lutheran Service Book* or *Lutheran Worship* (refer to hymnal index). (Note: Concordia Publishing House has available *The Concordia Organist.* All the initial worship hymns in the LifeLight courses are included in this resource. It's especially helpful for mission congregations and small parishes. See the list of study resources on page 7.) Follow with this prayer:

Prayer

O Lord Jesus, our Advocate with the Father, who stands in the breach of judgment for us and in our place, mercifully hear our prayers and enter not into judgment with Your servants. For the very thought of our sin causes us to hide from Your word of wrath. Grant us contrite and repentant hearts, that we may ever trust in Your redeeming and all-satisfying work for us as You bore the full wrath of the Father for us. Hear us for the sake of Your gracious intercession on our behalf. In Your name we pray. Amen.

Lecture Presentation

1 Brought Up on Charges (Hosea 4:1)

Evening network television loves the courtroom. It seems that every season there's another crime/law investigative show filling our living rooms. It's exciting. Often, we see a battle for truth when all odds seem opposed. There's a wavering judge, a mixed jury, and equally adamant defense and prosecuting attorneys. We rejoice when the truth is revealed, when justice prevails—often on account of some judicial loophole.

As we enter this main section of prophecy in Hosea, we also enter the courtroom. However, in this court, the judge is steady and strict—He is God Himself: (Hosea 4:1) "The Lord has a controversy with the inhabitants of the land." The word we see as "controversy" (ESV) comes from the Hebrew word *rîb*. It appeared once already in Hosea 2:2, where we read: "Plead with your mother, plead." This "pleading" or "controversy" might better be translated as "charge," as in "The Lord has a *charge* against the inhabitants of the land." Although God the Father is ultimately the judge, He has also appointed a plaintiff who draws up charges against Israel—that's Hosea. This sort of charge is central to the prophecy of Hosea, but it isn't unique to him. We find similar accusations hurled against God's people throughout the prophets, even in the Book of the Twelve. For example, Micah proclaims: (6:1–2)

> Hear what the Lord says:
> Arise, plead your case [rîb] before the mountains,
> and let the hills hear your voice.
> Hear, you mountains, the indictment [rîb] of the Lord,
> and you enduring foundations of the earth,
> for the Lord has an indictment [rîb] against His people,
> and He will contend with Israel.

But why does our Lord draw up charges against His people Israel? Well, for two reasons: things Israel has omitted and things Israel has committed. Much like us, Israel both neglected things she should have done as well as did all sorts of things she shouldn't have. Hosea is clear on this indictment: Israel has omitted faithfulness, mercy, and knowledge. Instead, she has committed swearing, lying, murdering, stealing, and adultery—that is, idolatry (4:1–2).

These charges have already been shown forth in the life of Hosea and his wife, Gomer. The charges against Gomer, which depict those spoken here against Israel, were laid in Hosea 2:2. Israel is the Lord's unfaithful wife. These are the grounds for divorce. This is what we'd call a stern preaching of the Law—the sins of Israel are shown for what they really are: an assault on the love of God. This charge—against the Northern Kingdom of Israel—will be laid once more in Hosea against the Kingdom of Judah in the south (12:2). Together, these show the all-encompassing effect of sin, that "None is righteous, no, not one" (Romans 3:10).

2 Knowing God and Being Known by God (Hosea 4:4–6)

As the charges are first spoken, we come across some very important vocabulary, not only for Hosea's book of prophecy but also for the Scriptures as a whole. The things Israel lacks are foundational characteristics of Yahweh: faithfulness, mercy, knowledge. One of the famous Old Testament creeds declares of God: (Exodus 34:6) "The **Lord**, the **Lord**, a God merciful and gracious, slow to anger, and abounding in steadfast love and faithfulness." The Hebrew word for "faithfulness" here is the same as that for "truth"; in fact, it's the root of our "Amen." This is simply who God is. He is true, faithful, merciful, and kind.

But then there's that last word in Hosea 4:1: "no knowledge of God in the land." And a little later, in verse 6, Hosea famously says, "My people are destroyed for lack of knowledge; because you have rejected knowledge, I reject you." If faithfulness and mercy are attributes of who the Lord is, we would also expect the same of knowledge. The prophet Amos helps us to rightly see knowledge as something God has of us: (3:2) "You only have I known of all the families of the earth." God's knowledge of His people is sometimes translated into English as His "choosing." For instance, God "chose" Abraham, and yet the Hebrew says, "God knew Abraham" (Genesis 18:19). The same goes for Moses (Exodus 33:12, 17), David (2 Samuel 7:20), and Jeremiah (Jeremiah 1:5). We also see the Lord's knowledge of His people in Nahum: (1:7) "The Lord is good, a stronghold in the day of trouble; He knows those who take refuge in Him." Lastly, perhaps you are familiar with the prayer from Psalm 139:23–24: "Search me, O God, and know my heart! Try me and know my thoughts! And see if there be any grievous way in me, and lead me in the way everlasting!" Our Lord is a God who knows. He knows the thoughts and hearts of all mankind. His knowledge covers both our sin and our faith, our failures and our joys. He knows us.

That is where the indictment comes in: the God who knows us, who is faithful to us, who loves us with steadfast love and mercy, is the God we have rejected. There is no knowledge of Him, no faithfulness toward Him, no steadfast love of Him. The charge is that the marriage between the Lord and His people Israel has been broken not by God but by us. Israel has known other lovers. She no longer knows the Lord. This knowledge clearly surpasses a simple head-knowledge. It's not that she lacks information about God. It's that she has forgotten who He is for her. Knowledge here is a relationship, a union, an intimate bond. This knowledge pertains not just to the head but also the heart and the soul. What Israel lacks is the intimate relationship with the Lord: the fear, trust, and love in God above all things.

How did this come about? How did Israel forget God (Hosea 4:6b)? Throughout this section of Hosea, everyone is at fault. Prophet, priest, and king all bear the brunt of Hosea's charge. When the indictment rings out, it appears that one of the priests stands in opposition, or better, defense of Israel: (4:4) "Yet let no one contend, and let none accuse." Our English translation does not supply quotation marks, but this may be an interjection of the priest, possibly Amaziah (see Amos 7:10–13). The Lord then homes in on this priest and lays the charge against him. Why? Because, as a teacher of Israel, the priest has failed to pass on the teaching of the Lord (Hosea 4:6). In place of the doctrine of God, Israel has been drinking deeply of the doctrine of Baal.

3 He Who Has Ears to Hear, Let Him Hear! (Hosea 4–7:2)

The call that begins both chapters 4 and 5 is "Hear!" This is the same call that Israel is founded upon: (Deuteronomy 6:4) "Hear, O Israel: The Lord our God, the Lord is one." We sometimes refer to this by its Hebrew name: the *Shema*. Hosea calls Israel to hear the indictment, to hear the judgment for their sin, to hear the Word of the Lord. This call breaks into their midst like a load of bricks. It pierces the darkness they've come to love. It shakes their foundation as an earthquake. That's how our Lord's voice sounds when it enters the realm of sin. Israel's sin is evident by all sorts of symptoms. But like any illness, if we treat just the symptoms, there is no hope for a cure. The source and root of the sin must be attacked—that's where Hosea lays the charge. The source of Israel's sin is their replacement of Baal for the Lord. They have found a new lover, a new god, a new provider and protector and sustainer; or so they think.

Baal worship is the most pervasive and egregious idolatry we encounter in the Scriptures. Baal was regarded as the champion of the Canaanite gods. Wearing a helmet with bull horns, holding a spear and club in his hands, Baal was the god who promised fertility and life, both for the land as well as the family. He was given charge of the rain in its season, bringing forth new crops and therefore the livelihood of the people. But Baal was demanding. This annual ritual included things such as cult prostitution, child sacrifice, and nature worship (none of which were condoned by the Lord). An image associated with Baal was a golden bull calf, which King Jeroboam constructed at each of the shrines he established in the Northern Kingdom, one at Dan and one at Bethel, which Hosea often calls by its more nefarious name, Beth-aven: "house of wickedness" (4:15; 5:8; 10:5, 8).

Baal worship was evident throughout the prophecy of Hosea—however, it was often cryptic at best. For example, (4:2b) "They break all bounds, and bloodshed follows bloodshed." This most likely refers to the armed authorities sent by the Baal priesthood to break into homes and seize victims for sacrifice; they left behind them a trail of blood. Another example of child sacrifice comes in 5:2: "And the revolters have gone deep into slaughter." Child sacrifice is referred to also in Psalm 106:35–39 and Deuteronomy 32:15–21. Another symptom of Baalism is the worship of the creation as opposed to the creator. In Hosea 4:12, the Creator says, "My people inquire of a piece of wood, and their walking staff gives them oracles," rather than gathering around the Lord's Word at the mouth of the prophet. Their gatherings were at the high places "under oak, poplar, and terebinth" (4:13). This nature cult leads further down the path of destruction because of the cult prostitution rampant under the shade of these large trees: (4:14) "for the men themselves go aside with prostitutes and sacrifice with cult prostitutes"; hence the repetition that they have gone off to play the whore.

Baal worship was "officially" adopted under the reign of Jeroboam (the only Israelite king listed in Hosea 1:1). It became viral, however, under his successor Ahab and Ahab's wife Jezebel. For the historical account of this false worship, see 1 Kings 12–22. While Israel worshiped Baal, committing the blatant sin of idolatry against the First Commandment, they never worshiped Baal exclusively. Israel didn't want to deny the Lord outright, but they wanted to pick up Baal as well, hedging their bets and seeking counsel from both. This is what we call "syncretism." It was a joint worship service, bringing together two (or more) separate religious practices as if they were all in agreement. Israel thought she could keep the Lord and His doctrine pure while simply changing the style of her worship to reflect some of the Baal practices that surrounded her. Hosea issues the strong response "No!"

That is Hosea's call. (4:1) "Hear the word of the Lord"; (5:1) "Hear this, O priests! Pay attention, O house of Israel! Give ear, O house of the king! For the judgment is for you"; (5:8) "Blow the horn in Gibeah, the trumpet in Ramah. Sound the alarm at Beth-aven." Hosea wants all ears to hear, all mouths to be stopped, all idolatry to cease, all of Baal worship to come to an end. And in this call toward repentance, fierce words of judgment ring out:

> (4:5) You shall stumble by day;
> the prophet also shall stumble with you by night;
> and I will destroy your mother.
>
> (4:6) I also will forget your children.
>
> (4:9) I will punish them for their ways
> and repay them for their deeds.

Worst of all is perhaps that the Lord has removed His gracious presence from Israel (5:6). And instead of grace, they find the Lord (5:12, 14) "like a moth to Ephraim, and like dry rot to the house of Judah . . . like a lion to Ephraim, and like a young lion to the house of Judah." The Lord now is known to them only by His punishment and anger: (5:14b) "I, even I, will tear and go away; I will carry off, and no one shall rescue." That's the Lord Israel needed most, the one who would shake her from her complacency under Baal and bring her to feel and hate her sin.

We love conversion stories. We love a change of heart, the thought process behind repentance. But Hosea doesn't give us any of it. Nevertheless, he gives what is important: Israel repented! Hosea 6 begins with Israel's confession, both of sin and of faith: (vv. 1–3a)

> Come, let us return to the Lord;
> for He has torn us, that He may heal us;
> He has struck us down, and He will bind us up.
> After two days He will revive us;
> on the third day He will raise us up,
> that we may live before Him.
> Let us know; let us press on to know the Lord.

Repentance has two parts, and Israel has done both: admitted to her guilt and clung to God for her salvation. In this confession, we see a hidden prophecy of Christ's rest in the tomb and His resurrection on the third day. We also see the renewed desire for knowledge of the Lord—again, not simply head knowledge or facts—by the restored relationship between the Lord and His people.

4 Steeped in Politics (Hosea 7:3–10:15)

Israel's repentance was short lived. Amidst Hosea's onslaught, there is a breath of redemption in 6:1–4. But the next verse lands us back into the crushing words of the prophet. Then comes one of Hosea's most famous phrases, quoted frequently in the New Testament: (6:6) "For I desire steadfast love and not sacrifice, the knowledge of God rather than burnt offerings" (see also Matthew 9:13; 12:7).

Her lack of faith and desire for the quick and easy way of works has caused Israel more troubles than she knows. It leads to a big political mess! Chapter 7 likens the political situation to a baker who gets drunk, sleeps on the job, and fails to tend the fire, leading to a cake that is burnt, moldy, and useless. We must recall the political situation at that time: in a twelve-year span, four kings were assassinated in Israel (see 2 Kings 15).

So, what do the king and princes have to do with all this Baalism? Does Jeroboam really have his heart set on the golden bull or the cult prostitution or the child sacrifice? Probably not. What Jeroboam seeks, as do most rulers, is peace and control over his people by creating a self-sustaining cult in opposition to other lands. Jeroboam wanted to make the worship of Israel in the north a legitimate and independent attraction to replace worship at the temple that resided in Jerusalem down south. This rivalrous syncretistic worship is what Hosea repeatedly calls "the pride of Israel" (5:5; 7:10). It's this pride that hardens their hearts and keeps them firmly planted within Baalism, "the spirit of whoredom" (4:12; 5:4). This false worship has many political ramifications, one of which is Israel's seeking aid from foreign lands such as Egypt and Assyria (see Hosea 7:11). They seek Baal's help; but as Hosea points out, Baal is really not God, and seeking help from him makes them like a "treacherous bow" (7:16).

Chapter 8 highlights Israel's clear breaking of the covenant with the Lord and the judgment that must follow. First, they made king and rulers apart from the Lord's command (v. 4a). Second, it was their own hands that carved and formed their idol—hardly a god to be worshiped (v. 4b–6). Because of this, they are reaping what they have sown: famine, drought, devastation, and international scorn (v. 7b–10). And yet, in the midst of all her sin, Hosea pleads, (v. 5) "How long will they be incapable of innocence?" How long will she remain cut off from the place of forgiveness? How long will her pride hold on to these places of false worship and the idolatry of these false gods? How long will she reject the Word and will of the Lord—thinking His covenant a strange thing?

In the midst of such unfaithfulness, the Law of the Lord must do its work. Israel will again return to Egypt (Hosea 9:3). Egypt is the place of slavery, bondage, no-mercy. In words of somber judgment, Hosea declares: (9:1) "Rejoice not, O Israel! Exult not like the peoples." While this sorrow will be turned to joy later on in this Book of the Twelve (see Zephaniah 3:14; Zechariah 9:9), for now, this is the Word for Israel. Her offerings are rejected. Her land is shut up. The end-time punishment is spoken over Israel now—(9:7) "Israel shall know it."

If Israel has any chance for repentance, it will come from the prophet's voice alone. He alone delivers the Word of the Lord. He alone is given to declare them forgiven. But it is precisely the prophet that they reject. Hosea gives a bit of autobiographical data when he says, (9:7b–8)

> The prophet is a fool;
> the man of the spirit is mad,
> because of your great iniquity
> and great hatred.
> The prophet is the watchman of Ephraim with my God;
> yet a fowler's snare is on all his ways,
> and hatred in the house of his God.

Hosea calls himself a fool. Hosea is mad. Hosea, the watchman of Ephraim, is caught in a snare like a thief or a predator. That's how deep their corruption goes! They have become just like the thing they worship (9:10)—nothing!

They invested so much stock into Baal that they could see nothing else. They couldn't see how short-lived it would be. They couldn't see the coming destruction or the impotence of this false god. Hosea proclaims Baal's destruction as surely as if it were already accomplished: (10:8)

> The high places of Aven, the sin of Israel,
> shall be destroyed.
> Thorn and thistle shall grow up
> on their altars,
> and they shall say to the mountains, "Cover us,"
> and to the hills, "Fall on us."

Conclusion: A Change of Heart

But Hosea's anger subsides. A change comes that turns his fury into sadness and from sadness to pleading. You can hear the earnestness in Hosea's words:(10:12)

> Sow for yourself righteousness;
> reap steadfast love;
> break up your fallow ground,
> for it is the time to seek the Lord,
> that He may come and rain righteousness upon you.

This is reminiscent of the turn in Hosea's pleading for Gomer (2:13–14). It reveals the true motive behind our Lord's Word of the Law: His love for His people. The Lord never speaks His word of Law for the sake of the Law and destruction alone. It is always for the sake of the Gospel, always for the restoration and love of His people.

The sentiment of love reminds the Lord of His own work of deliverance: (11:1) "When Israel was a child, I loved him, and out of Egypt I called My son." Chapter 11 appears to be like a conversation within the Lord's own mind. Here He reconsiders all that has been said up until now. In a sense, God repents. He turns from His judgment. He quits expecting Israel to turn, and He turns them. He remembers teaching Ephraim to walk (v. 3) and the reins of love He used to guide his childhood and development (v. 4). The Lord's own inner turmoil erupts with His self-questioning and His response of faithfulness: (vv. 8–9)

> How can I give you up, O Ephraim?
> How can I hand you over, O Israel? . . .
> My heart recoils within Me;
> My compassion grows warm and tender.
> I will not execute My burning anger;
> I will not again destroy Ephraim;
> for I am God and not a man,
> the Holy One in your midst,
> and I will not come in wrath.

That's who our Lord is. He is the God who acts—the God who remembers His own love and His own faithfulness and His own knowledge of His people. While Israel only rejected and rejected all the time, seeking another lover in Baal, it was our Lord's resolute pursuit of love that brought Israel back.

Matthew's Gospel famously quotes Hosea 11:1 as fulfilled in Christ's return from Egypt as a young boy. That episode mirrors this preaching extraordinarily well. When Herod raged against the Holy Innocents, an angel appeared to Joseph and guided him to Egypt. The joy of the birth of the Savior was quickly dampened by the slaughter of all male children two years old and younger. Jesus, who would save His people from their sin, was led away from the people, back into Egypt, into slavery. But because of God's great mercy, "Out of Egypt I called My Son" (Matthew 2:15). It was mercy that brought the Christ Child back to Israel. It was mercy that led the people of Israel by Moses' hand into the wilderness and with Joshua into the Promised Land. It was mercy that again caused the Lord to have a change of heart—He will not come in wrath.

Concluding Activities

Conclude the session with an appropriate prayer and distribute the study leaflet for week 4.

The Fear of the Lord Is the Beginning of Wisdom

Hosea 11:12–14:9

Preparing for the Session

Central Focus

Hosea ends his introduction to the Book of the Twelve with a call to wisdom. We are truly wise in recognizing who God is and what God has done for us, and in trusting Him to do it again and again!

Objectives

That participants, led by the Holy Spirit working through God's Word, will

1. wrestle with some of the textual difficulties presented in Hosea;
2. apply God's charge against Israel to their own lives;
3. interpret God's dealing with them in light of who He is for them; and
4. hear God's voice to them in the preaching and teaching of their pastors.

Note for the small-group leaders: Lesson notes and other materials you will need begin on page 62.

For the Lecture Leader

Session Plan

Worship

Begin the session with the hymn printed in the study leaflet. Accompaniments are available in denominational hymnals, such as *Lutheran Service Book* or *Lutheran Worship* (refer to hymnal index). (Note: Concordia Publishing House has available *The Concordia Organist*. All the initial worship hymns in the LifeLight courses are included in this resource. It's especially helpful for mission congregations and small parishes. See the list of study resources on page 7.) Follow with this prayer:

Prayer

"O come Thou Wisdom from on high, who ord'rest all things mightily; To us the path of knowledge show, and teach us in her ways to go." Amen. (*LSB* 357:2)

Lecture Presentation

1 Ephraim and Judah—Two of a Kind (Hosea 11:12)

In some ways, families are the same everywhere. For whatever reason, if the oldest child is scolded for doing something she shouldn't be doing, the younger child tries it also. The reaction is the same, or worse, every time: "I just told your sister, 'No!' Why did *you* do it too?" The more time one spends as a parent, the more one sympathizes with God as Father.

As we come to the close of Hosea, we see that the sin of Ephraim (the Northern Kingdom) has spread its way into Judah (the Southern Kingdom), despite warnings by the prophet: (4:15) "Though you play the whore, O Israel, let not Judah become guilty." The translations here are a bit confusing as we finish off chapter 11. Some translations have interpreted Hosea 11:12 to present Judah in a negative light, but the majority display Judah favorably. Compare the NASB with the ESV below.

NASB:

> Judah is also unruly against God,
> Even against the Holy One who is faithful.

ESV:

> But Judah still walks with God
> and is faithful to the Holy One.

The difference in meaning between these is night and day. If we read with the ESV a distinction between Ephraim and Judah—the one good, the other bad—then two verses later (12:2), we're in even more of a mess: "The Lord has an indictment [charge; *rîb*] against Judah." Why would the Lord make charges against Judah if Hosea just told us that, unlike Ephraim, they held fast to Him? The Hebrew text here is equally unclear, so the context seems to make most sense reading this as though Judah has committed Ephraim's crime. She did just as her sister, even though she saw her scolded for it. She failed to hear the Lord's Word and cling to His promises. Like Ephraim, she "feeds on the wind" (12:1) of whoredom, lusting after false gods such as Baal. Rather than seeking all good in the Lord alone (Mark 10:18), the people of Judah run to Assyria and Egypt for help. For the same crime as her sister, Judah is now indicted by the Lord. What can we now say about Judah and Ephraim? Not only are the differences between these countries of less significance than we may have earlier thought but the kingdoms truly are two peas in a pod.

2 Jacob and the Prophets (Hosea 12)

Once the indictment is laid against Judah, a new character is introduced: Jacob. The question for us to consider now is whether Jacob here is good or bad. In considering that, we should ask why it is that Hosea calls to mind all these old allusions to the Jacob stories in Genesis. And to whom does the reference to "Jacob" refer anyhow—the patriarch from the Book of Genesis or the Southern Kingdom of Judah? Or could it perhaps refer to both? In just a few verses, Hosea alludes to six different episodes of Jacob's story in Genesis; but are these examples for Judah to follow or are they evidence of the people's sin? After we take a closer look at these, we will ask what Hosea intends to accomplish with them.

The first allusion Hosea makes is to the birth of Jacob and Esau from Genesis 25:26, where Jacob gets his name as the "heel-grabber." Then Hosea tells of Jacob's striving with God: (12:4) "He strove with the angel and prevailed." This recalls Jacob's visit and wrestling match with the stranger at the Jabbok (Genesis 32:22–32). In both of these allusions, it might be easy to mistake Jacob's actions as impious or sinful. And yet, in reading the stories from Genesis, we find out that, rather than being condemned by God, Jacob was actually blessed by God. The relationship between Jacob and Esau was poor at best; but, as the Lord reminds us in Malachi 1:2, "Yet I have loved Jacob but Esau I have hated." And what about that wrestling match at the Jabbok—isn't it wrong to wrestle with God? Well, not according to the Book of Genesis! Jacob receives a blessing for his striving with this "man," whom Hosea calls both God and an angel. How should we regard this unusual event? Perhaps it is not quite as unusual as we think. After all, is this not also what prayer is primarily about—wrestling with God and laying before Him our requests and intercessions, holding Him to His promise to hear and bless? We all wrestle with God at times, in a sense, as we bring our concerns before Him and plead for His mercy—and we each are blessed, as Jacob was before us.

According to the accounts in Genesis, Jacob is presented as a noble patriarch, the father of the tribes of Israel. Hosea's charge against the Jacob of the day, the Southern Kingdom, is that they aren't acting like Jacob of old. They no longer call out and wrestle with God—they have bowed down to Baal and worshiped him, just as Ephraim in the North did. That's why the ultimate call of Hosea is a call toward repentance: (12:6) "So you, by the help of your God, return, hold fast to love and justice, and wait continually for your God."

However, repentance cannot come without the word of the prophets. Judah cannot turn from the ways of Ephraim without hearing the prophetic call. This is why Hosea then emphasizes the role of the prophets in 12:10–14. The prophets are our Lord's mouthpieces. We can recall that Jacob was the Lord's prophet to his wife Rachel, serving for her and, with her, fleeing from the land of Aram. Later on, Moses acted as the Lord's prophet to the people of Israel, serving for years in Egypt and then fleeing with them. In both of these instances, it is our Lord who delivered His people by the hand of the prophets. And Hosea's point is that God is doing the same now by Hosea's prophetic preaching—delivering them through the call to repentance and the promise of God's mercy and forgiveness.

3 The Sting of Death (Hosea 13)

In confirmation class, children learn that the Law of God shows us our sin. The Law kills; it gives no hope. It points out the reality of sin without offering any comfort or means of salvation. Therefore, we can say that the Law ultimately kills. That is Hosea's word to unrepentant Israel. He again teaches them the First Commandment: (13:4) "Know no God but Me, and besides Me there is no savior" (see Exodus 20:3). That Word brings guilt upon Israel because they have many gods, even setting up the worship of Baal and the Lord side by side. Therefore, God must come to them in the way of the Law: (Hosea 13:7–8) "So I am to them like a lion; like a leopard I will lurk beside the way. I will fall upon them like a bear robbed of her cubs; I will tear open their breast, and there I will devour them like a lion, as a wild beast would rip them open."

We have come across this animal imagery of destruction before, earlier in our study (5:14). We have also heard of our Lord's slaying words of judgment (6:5). Again,

Hosea cries out: (13:9) "He destroys you, O Israel, for you are against Me, against your helper." When God is against you, what do you do? To whom can you flee for refuge? Where can you find safety or defense? We're reminded of David's cries in Psalm 139:7–8:

> Where shall I go from Your Spirit?
> Or where shall I flee from Your presence?
> If I ascend to heaven, You are there!
> If I make my bed in Sheol, You are there!

We can even recall how, when Job found himself in this same situation, he cried out: (Job 31:35) "Oh, that I had one to hear me!" Both David and Job need an advocate with God. There is no one who is able to withstand the Lord's accusations, His charge against His people, unless he has an advocate with the Father. That is the Gospel that John proclaims: (1 John 2:1–2) "My little children, . . . we have an advocate with the Father, Jesus Christ the righteous. He is the propitiation for our sins, and not for ours only but also for the sins of the whole world." No king or carved idol will plead our case before the Father—only Jesus can and will. And so, when Hosea speaks the Lord's words of judgment, we know to find their reversal only in Christ: (13:14)

> Shall I ransom them from the power of Sheol?
> Shall I redeem them from Death?
> O Death, where are your plagues?
> O Sheol, where is your sting?

This section of Hosea, spoken in judgment, finds its reversal in the cross of Christ. Paul says, (1 Corinthians 15:54–57)

> When the perishable puts on the imperishable, and the mortal puts on immortality, then shall come to pass the saying that is written:
>
> "Death is swallowed up in victory."
> "O death, where is your victory?
> O death, where is your sting?"
>
> The sting of death is sin, and the power of sin is the law. But thanks be to God, who gives us the victory through our Lord Jesus Christ.

Israel is ransomed from death and the power of the devil by the work of Jesus. And that work of Christ comes to the people of Judah through the preaching of the prophets, the preaching of repentance. In their repentance is the sure and certain promise of forgiveness from God. For as God has promised to send a Savior into the world, in Him they are forgiven forever. Even though they would each die, being forgiven in the Christ who was promised to come, they will have that unfailing victory over death and the grave: life everlasting.

4 Repent, for the Kingdom of Heaven Is Near! (Hosea 14:1–7)

All repentance has its source in the Lord; it is never something we churn up within ourselves. Repentance is a passive thing—our Lord repents us. We are turned. We are changed. We are brought near. It's all Him for us. That's what it means for the Lord to be "the Holy One in your midst" (Hosea 11:9). He is the actor; He is the worker; He is the doer of our repentance. And we, Israel, are those who are repented, turned, changed, forgiven. Consider how this is phrased in the Augsburg Confession, one of the Lutheran confessional documents: "Repentance consists of two parts. One part is contrition, that is, terrors striking the conscience through the knowledge of sin. The other part is faith, which is born of the Gospel [Romans 10:17]" (AC XII 3–5).

In this way, Hosea begins chapter 14: "Return, O Israel, to the Lord your God, for you have stumbled because of your iniquity. Take with you words and return to the Lord." Here we have a clear call to repentance—a call for them both to acknowledge their sin (because of their iniquity) and also to trust in the Lord's forgiveness (holding before Him His words, or promises). The second part of Hosea 14:2 might be understood as meaning "*You* take away all iniquity." It is a confession; it is a statement of faith. This great profession of faith is then followed by confessing the impotence and worthlessness of Baal and of all the surrounding nations: (14:3)

> Assyria shall not save us;
> we will not ride on horses;
> and we will say no more, "Our God,"
> to the work of our hands.

This repentance—both parts—is ultimately the work of the Lord. And to this repentance, our gracious God responds with more promises (14:4–7). It is the Lord who heals; it is the Lord who loves; it is the Lord who turns His anger. It is the Lord who again gives rain and dew and growth and fruit. It is the Lord who gives life and beauty and joy. It is the Lord who again weds His Bride and washes her with rebirth and renewal (refer to Titus 3:5). That is the life of repentance that we have with our heavenly Bridegroom, Jesus Christ (Ephesians 5:32).

Conclusion: Wise Endings (Hosea 14:9)

We have already discussed how the knowledge of God plays a major role in the prophecy of Hosea. This was the original charge (or indictment) against Israel: (4:1) "There is . . . no knowledge of God in the land." This was also the charge against Hosea's wife, Gomer, who typifies Israel: (2:8) "She did not know that it was I who gave her the grain, the wine, and the oil, and who lavished on her silver and gold, which they used for Baal." And most recently, in 13:6, we heard again that Israel "forgot Me," which is why the Lord must stand as a wild beast against them, tearing them with the Word of judgment. But in all of this lack of knowledge, God still knows His people: (13:5) "It was I who knew you in the wilderness, in the land of drought." The Lord our God never forgets. He never knows other lovers. He never forsakes His first love. This is what Israel must know. They must know who God is and what He is like for them! And this is how the Book of Hosea draws to a close: (14:9)

> Whoever is wise, let him understand these things;
> whoever is discerning, let him know them;
> for the ways of the Lord are right,
> and the upright walk in them,
> but transgressors stumble in them.

True wisdom is having the knowledge of God—it is knowing God. And, as we said earlier, this isn't merely a kind of head-knowledge or an accumulation of facts about God; rather, it is knowing God intimately, as a bride knows her husband. It is a knowledge that is marked by fear, love, and trust.

This is how Moses desired to know God as well. So Moses said, "Please, let me know Your ways that I may know You" (Exodus 33:13, the author's translation). Notice how Moses associates the knowledge of God with the ways of God. To know God is to know His ways, to know what He is like. It is to know His character as the Holy One of Israel. Knowing the ways of the Lord is to know the Lord Himself. So how does one know the ways of the Lord? Well, only by the Word of the Lord—the words spoken by the mouth of the prophet. Only through them can one hear and know the deeds of the Lord. That's the point of Hosea: Israel does not know the Lord because she has ceased to hear His Word; she has rejected His prophets.

But if Israel were to hear the prophets—if she were to listen and repent and trust the words of their mouths—what would she hear? What would the ways of the Lord be like? Later in this Book of the Twelve, Micah (7:18–20) says,

> Who is a God like You, pardoning iniquity
> and passing over transgression
> for the remnant of His inheritance?
> He does not retain His anger forever,
> because He delights in steadfast love.
> He will again have compassion on us;
> He will tread our iniquities underfoot.
> You will cast all our sins
> into the depths of the sea.
> You will show faithfulness to Jacob
> and steadfast love to Abraham,
> as You have sworn to our fathers
> from the days of old.

That is what God is like; those are His ways. He is the forgiving God. He is the God of mercy and compassion. He is the God of great reversals. He is the God who takes back sinful Gomer and adulterous Israel and promiscuous Judah. He runs after His own and washes them clean in the blood of the Lamb. He speaks His Word of forgiveness and makes them holy, as He is holy.

The conclusion to the Book of Hosea assumes there will be readers and hearers beyond those Israelites of Hosea's day. It is a call to all—a call of repentance and a call of faith; in other words, it is a call of wisdom for you. Hosea invites us all to hear and know the ways of the Lord and thereby to know God Himself. "The ways of the Lord," Hosea says, "are right" (14:9). That means they are true and trustworthy; they can be believed. The wise are those who believe that the Lord is the God He claims to be. They are those who recognize His works and delight in them. The wicked, however, are those who think these great works come from other lovers, other gods.

Dear Lord, enable us always to see and know, hear and believe Your Word and Your works. Or, as the Psalms say, (25:4–5)

> Make me to know Your ways, O Lord;
> teach me Your paths.
> Lead me in Your truth and teach me,
> for You are the God of my salvation;
> for You I wait all the day long.

Concluding Activities

Conclude the session with an appropriate prayer and distribute the study leaflet for week 5.

Judgment: Despair or Hope?

Joel 1:1–2:11

Preparing for the Session

Central Focus

The judgment described in the first half of Joel is a plague/word/cross that appears in each and every life. As this Word is executed, those who cling to their sin find only despair; but for those who receive the work of this cross in faith, there is only hope—leading to life everlasting.

Objectives

That participants, led by the Holy Spirit working through God's Word, will

1. understand the complexity of Scripture in general and the unique witness of Joel in particular;
2. compare the suffering of the locust invasion to the various crosses they bear today;
3. interpret the prophetic Last Day in full view of the crucifixion of Christ the Lord; and
4. live for the Lord, anticipating His return.

Note for the small-group leaders: Lesson notes and other materials you will need begin on page 64.

For the Lecture Leader

Session Plan

Worship

Begin the session with the hymn printed in the study leaflet. Accompaniments are available in denominational hymnals, such as *Lutheran Service Book* or *Lutheran Worship* (refer to hymnal index). (Note: Concordia Publishing House has available *The Concordia Organist.* All the initial worship hymns in the LifeLight courses are included in this resource. It's especially helpful for mission congregations and small parishes. See the list of study resources on page 7.) Follow with this prayer:

Prayer

O Suffering Servant, who executed Your Word in time by the preaching of the prophets, and who, as the Word Incarnate, underwent the execution of the cross for us, come again quickly—not in wrath or judgment but in grace and abundant mercy. For You are slow to anger, ever patient with us in our sin, and always abounding in steadfast love. In Your name we pray. Amen.

Lecture Presentation

1 Joel: A Person and a Book (Joel 1:1)

Any good detective knows that facts come in the questioning: who, what, where, and when? From these questions, one can determine a motive and explanation—the how and the why. When we bring these questions to certain biblical texts, we readily find dates and times and locations. But then there are others, like Joel, that resist any such certainty of facts. All we get with Joel is that he is "the son of Pethuel" (1:1), which doesn't necessarily help us identify Joel, since we can't be sure whether Pethuel is Joel's father, grandfather, or notable ancestor. Sure, some clues pop up here and there, but we are never exactly sure what to make of them.

So, who is this Joel? Martin Luther says of him: "Joel was a kindly and gentle man" (AE 35:318). Nothing in the Scriptures says such a thing, but Luther rightly understands this based on what Joel has said. And as far as our knowledge of Joel goes, it seems we have facts about little more than what he has preached.

Now, there are other Joels in Scripture, but no clear word that ties any of them together with this Joel. Samuel's firstborn son is a Joel, but we're told that he didn't "walk in [Samuel's] ways but turned aside after gain" (1 Samuel 8:3). Another Joel is one of the eighth-century descendents of Simeon, a wealthy prince of his clan (1 Chronicles 4:35). The name Joel, which means "The Lord is God," appears in various genealogies and lists of names, but none speak explicitly of a prophet. Also of little help is the fact that nowhere else in Scripture do we come across Pethuel, Joel's father.

Dating Joel is just as problematic. Scholars are so divided on the dating of Joel that some place him and his book in the ninth century BC, while others are convinced he preached or wrote in the second century BC. Subtle hints in the text don't give us much certainty, but they do suggest a probable dating somewhere between the mid-eighth century and the early sixth century, depending largely upon whom he addresses in this short book of prophecy. While Hosea and Amos both address the Northern Kingdom explicitly, Joel may be addressing Judah in the South. His letter is full of temple imagery and liturgical actions and rites, and he mentions both Judah and Jerusalem by name (3:1). Such temple talk suggests that the temple was still around when Joel's prophecy was put to writing—so it's at least before 587 BC. And because Joel mentions the "Valley of Jehoshaphat" (3:2), he must be preaching after Jehoshaphat reigned as king (873–848 BC)—likely, long enough after his reign so that a valley is known by Jehoshaphat's name.

So what does all this uncertainty mean? Well, it's a gentle reminder that the Bible's primary concern is not with history per se—the simple recounting of dates and times—but with the story of God for man. Although God always relates to man in real time and in real place, there are many instances in the Scriptures where the times and the places distract us from the meat of the story. Indeed, there are times when dates and times and places are intentionally avoided so that the events can be easily understood in all times and all places for all people. Perhaps the preaching of Joel is the same way.

And what about the book named after Joel—what do we know about this? In the Hebrew Bible (and therefore our English translations as well) the Book of Joel follows the Book of Hosea and comes before Amos. But in the ancient Greek translation of the Old Testament, Joel follows Micah; the order is Hosea, Amos, Micah, Joel, Obadiah, Jonah, Nahum, Habakkuk, Zephaniah, Haggai, Zechariah, Malachi. What this suggests is that by being placed between Hosea and Amos, regardless of the date, Joel is meant to be read in that same context. While Hosea ends with a call to repentance, we as readers are left hanging, wondering whether the people repented or not. Joel helps by beginning his book with another call to repent. This call to repentance then turns into an end-times judgment against the nations, which is how Amos begins his work, with a series of oracles against the nations. Among other literary and theological links between these two books, Joel seems to fit well snuggled between them, and perhaps also within a context of the mid-late eighth century.

2 Locust Invasion! (Joel 1:2–12)

Have you ever talked with an old Kansan or Oklahoman about life in the Dust Bowl? The stories are quite amazing. One gentleman recalled how they had to bring their rakes and shovels in the house because the locusts were eating the wooden handles. Another said she remembered her dad mowing the lawn—not because it was growing too long but because it was covered by thousands upon thousands of locusts. Sure, they remember the heat and the famine and the suffering—but they all remember the locusts! In fact, for someone having lived through this era of American history, even reading this passage in Joel might bring many painful and vivid images to mind—some might relate a bit too well!

Joel begins his preaching with a warning, a call to arms, a sense of urgency. What is upon them now is unlike anything they've seen or heard before. This invasion of locusts is so destructive and all encompassing that nothing is spared from their appetite. Joel says, (1:4)

> What the cutting locust left,
> the swarming locust has eaten.
> What the swarming locust left,
> the hopping locust has eaten,
> and what the hopping locust left,
> the destroying locust has eaten.

So what are these locusts? What does Joel mean? Is he simply describing the bug infestation, or is there something more here? Do the locusts symbolize or represent an army invasion, either past, present, or future?

Things would be bad enough if it was just a bug. Even "just a bug" is nonsensical! Such a plague of locusts would destroy the people's crops, commerce, celebrations, meals, offerings, joy, and livelihood. Their worship and prayers were intimately tied to their land; and their land was intimately tied to the promise of the Lord. For the locusts to come and ravage the earth is to have God going against His Word of promise, and bringing forth His Word of judgment. These locusts, as a Word of judgment, call to mind also the eighth plague that was sent upon Egypt by the hand of Moses (Exodus 10:1–20).

Throughout the Church's reading of Joel, however, the locusts have often been understood to be more than locusts. Some have suggested that the four types of locusts (cutting, swarming, hopping, destroying) represent four kingdoms: the Egyptians, Babylonians, Assyrians, and Greeks/Romans. While we're not given to name names here, we might rightly understand these locusts both as literal destructive bugs and also as types or forerunners for a destructive army approaching the unrepentant inhabitants of the land.

If Joel is rightly to be read in the context of Hosea and Amos, then perhaps we could tie the locusts to the Assyrian invasion of 722 BC. Joel does suggest that we understand the locusts as something more than an infestation of bugs: (1:6) "For a nation has come up against my land, powerful and beyond number." And again he says, (2:2) "Like blackness there is spread upon the mountains a great and powerful people; their like has never been before, nor will be again after them through the years of all generations." But again, the problem with labeling the locusts is that Joel here intentionally allows for this destructive word to apply at all times and in all places. This "plague" is equally destructive during the Assyrian invasion as well as the Babylonian one. These locusts make their way even into the judgment scene of Revelation during the blowing of the seven trumpets: (9:3–4, 7–9)

> Then from the smoke came locusts on the earth, and they were given power like the power of scorpions of the earth. They were told not to harm the grass of the earth or any green plant or any tree, but only those people who do not have the seal of God on their foreheads. . . . In appearance the locusts were like horses prepared for battle: on their heads were what looked like crowns of gold; their faces were like human faces, their hair like women's hair, and their teeth like lions' teeth; they had breastplates like breastplates of iron, and the noise of their wings was like the noise of many chariots with horses rushing into battle.

3 My Vine and My Fig Tree (Joel 1:7)

So what do the locusts destroy? Whether bugs or armies, Joel says that destruction has come "against my land. . . . It has laid waste my vine and splintered my fig tree" (1:6a, 7a). Vines and fig trees are sort of a big deal for Israel. Indeed, Isaiah famously sings a love song about a vineyard (Isaiah 5). In that passage, the vineyard is a metaphor for Israel, and the vinedresser for the Lord. God cared so much for Israel that He dug around it, watered it, cared for it, protected it, and fed it all sorts of nutrients; yet the vine produced only wild grapes (i.e., inedible or poisonous grapes). Isaiah explains: (5:7) "For the vineyard of the Lord of hosts is the house of Israel, and the men of Judah are His pleasant planting; and He looked for justice, but behold, bloodshed; for righteousness, but behold, an outcry!" As the locusts strip the trees bare and the plants of their fruit, so also will the enemies of Israel strip Israel of her unrepentant fruit. The Lord works through them to prune the lives of His people.

The vine and fig tree carry on their metaphor into the New Testament as an image of the Church. Jesus says as much in John's Gospel: (15:1–6)

> I am the true vine, and My Father is the vinedresser. Every branch in Me that does not bear fruit He takes away, and every branch that does bear fruit He prunes, that it may bear more fruit. Already you are clean because of the word that I have spoken to you. Abide in Me, and I in you. As the branch cannot bear fruit by itself, unless it abides in the vine, neither can you, unless you abide in Me. I am the vine; you are the branches. Whoever abides in Me and I in him, he it is that bears much fruit, for apart from Me you can do nothing. If anyone does not abide in Me he is thrown away like a branch and withers; and the branches are gathered, thrown into the fire, and burned.

Luke records for us the parable of the barren fig tree: (13:6–9)

> A man had a fig tree planted in his vineyard, and he came seeking fruit on it and found none. And he said to the vinedresser, "Look, for three years now I have come seeking fruit on this fig tree, and I find none. Cut it down. Why should it use up the ground?" And he answered him, "Sir, let it alone this year also, until I dig around it and put on manure. Then if it should bear fruit next year, well and good; but if not, you can cut it down."

The fig tree in the parable represents the Church. Without fruit, it will be cut down. But as long as it is "in Christ," as John's Gospel says, then it will bear fruit and be saved. The fruit, however, is not the cause of it being saved but the result. A healthy, living tree naturally produces fruit. So it is here in Joel as well. The Lord's vine and fig tree are being ransacked by locusts because they lack repentance—or as John the Baptizer puts it, they lack "fruit in keeping with repentance" (Matthew 3:8).

4 Repent! The Day Is Surely Drawing Near (Joel 1:13–2:11)

We've looked at Hosea's call to repentance already. Joel's is much the same. So it goes for all the prophets—Israel must repent of her idolatry and cling to the promise of God alone. She is stuck in the stupor of her drunkenness (Joel 1:5). Complacent, sinfully at ease, unrepentant—Israel has lived as if God did not matter, and as if she mattered most. Therefore, Joel must splash the cold water, turn on the lights, and shout in the ear of sleepy Judah: "Repent!" He calls for lamentation and fasting, mourning and weeping, and a solemn assembly of repentance in the temple liturgy: (1:13)

> Put on sackcloth and lament, O priests;
> wail, O ministers of the altar.
> Go in, pass the night in sackcloth,
> O ministers of my God!

The call to repentance is a call to prayer, confession of sin, and faith. All three come together with repentance. Prayer is that open dialogue with God, saying back to Him what He has first said to us. It's a begging for mercy, a petition for a different outcome, a change of heart in God. The confession of sins is the admission of guilt, the awareness of sin, the neglect of God and His will. Faith is the trust that God will be who God is: (2:13) "gracious and merciful, slow to anger, and abounding in steadfast love."

Joel ties this call of repentance to the destruction of the locusts in the context of the Day of the Lord: (1:15) "Alas for the day! For the day of the LORD is near, and as destruction from the Almighty it comes." At the beginning of our study of the Book of the Twelve, we saw that this "day of the LORD" is what ties the Book of the Twelve together most strongly. It's a day of both judgment and acquittal, of grace and punishment, of Law and Gospel. To those perishing, the Day of the Lord is utterly fearful. As it is written in Revelation, (6:17) "The great day of their wrath has come, and who can stand?"

Surely, no sinner can stand before the Lord and live. As Paul says, (2 Corinthians 6:14) "What fellowship has light with darkness?" Likewise, Israel is unable to stand before the Lord and live. Therefore, Joel must be her prophet; he must intercede with and for her: (1:19) "To you, O LORD, I call." As the day approaches with "darkness and gloom" (2:2), "fire," "chariots," "weapons," and earthquakes (2:3, 5, 8, 10), the greatest judgment comes by the Lord's Word: (2:11) "The LORD utters His voice before His army. . . . He who executes His word is powerful."

Conclusion: The Word Executed

The Christian calendar traditionally begins and ends each year with a focus on this day. Advent prepares us for the coming of Christ—not only in the flesh, as at Christmas but also in glory on the Last Day. In fact, Advent envelopes three unique comings of Christ: in time (incarnation), in glory (second coming), and in grace (sacramental). The end of the Church Year, notably the last two or three Sundays of the Church Year, also prepares us for the coming of Christ. Traditional readings center on the Day of the Lord.

Our world today is full of a lot of rubbish when it comes to talk of the end, or the Last Day. There's about a million ways to get it wrong. We go wrong when we get the calculator out and start crunching numbers, trying to find out when that day will be; for "concerning that day or that hour, no one knows, not even the angels in heaven, nor the Son, but only the Father" (Mark 13:32). We go wrong when we dabble with all the relatively recent rapture ideas and the various forms of millennialism afloat today. We go wrong when we try to see today's political movements and powers as specifically foretold in Scripture. But perhaps the most deadly way to go wrong is to talk about the end apart from the cross of Jesus Christ.

Everything is finished on the cross. Ultimately, that is the Last Day, the Day of the Lord, Judgment Day. It's the cross that Joel is primarily describing here. The plague of locusts is but a shadow of the judgment that was laid upon the Son of God. The destruction of vine and fig tree was a picture of the destruction of the temple, the body of Christ. The darkness and gloom, the cosmic upheaval, the earthquake and trembling of heaven—all of these gather together at the cross. Matthew's Gospel gives us the most detail here: the rending of the temple curtain, the darkness, the shaking of the earth, the tombs opening, and the bodies rising. All of it occurring because, on the cross, God dies. The judgment is rendered. Sin is paid for.

Joel rhetorically asks, (2:11) "For the day of the LORD is great and very awesome; who can endure it?" No one can endure such a day; no one except God Himself, Jesus the Christ. Hanging on the cross, with nails piercing His hands and feet, a crown of thorns pressing into His head, and lash marks bleeding down His back, Jesus bears the Day of the Lord for us! That's what Joel is prophesying. And, along with Joel, so also declare all the prophets of God. They know and speak only what they see and hear. And what is revealed to them is the fullness of the divine plan, the redemption of man, the day of God's recompense. That's what Israel was to believe in their repentance—that God would be who God is. And, as Christians, we know who God is most fully by seeing Him crucified for us.

As Joel brings this first admonition to an end with the words "he who executes His word is powerful" (2:11), we are meant to consider the One who truly does execute the Word of God, who brings it about, who keeps it wholly and without defilement. We are to consider Jesus. And when we consider Jesus, we consider not only His keeping of the Lord's word faithfully for us—executing the commands perfectly, fulfilling the Law for us—but also the execution of the Word, the crucifixion of the Word made flesh. This is what makes that day so great and awesome: that God would bear the punishment Himself, in our place, for us, and grant us forgiveness in His Son, Jesus. That event alone turns this day of judgment from despair to hope.

Concluding Activities

Conclude the session with an appropriate prayer and distribute the study leaflet for week 6.

God for Us

Joel 2:12–3:21

Preparing for the Session

Central Focus

When everything in life seems hopeless, when all seems lost, when the time is up and the end is near—there's always Christ for you!

Objectives

That participants, led by the Holy Spirit working through God's Word, will

1. delight in the literary transition from death to life that Joel provides;

2. apply the moment of salvation provided for Israel to themselves;

3. come to defend the many ways in which God is gracious to His people of all times, even in the Old Testament; and

4. live by the Spirit each day.

Note for the small-group leaders: Lesson notes and other materials you will need begin on page 66.

For the Lecture Leader

Session Plan

Worship

Begin the session with the hymn printed in the study leaflet. Accompaniments are available in denominational hymnals, such as *Lutheran Service Book* or *Lutheran Worship* (refer to hymnal index). (Note: Concordia Publishing House has available *The Concordia Organist*. All the initial worship hymns in the LifeLight courses are included in this resource. It's especially helpful for mission congregations and small parishes. See the list of study resources on page 7.) Follow with this prayer:

Prayer

O Incarnate Savior, who stepped down from Your mighty and timeless throne above into the thicket of time and place here below, draw us back to Your eternal home—even in the last hour when all seems lost—for with Your salvation the time is always meet, right, and salutary. In Your name we pray. Amen.

Lecture Presentation

1 Introduction: On the Brink of Destruction (Joel 2:7–11)

Every movie has a turning point, every book a climax, every story pivots—sometimes even on a single word. Joel's book of prophecy is no different. Chapter 1 and the first eleven verses of chapter 2 sound the alarm of judgment. Joel calls the elders of the people to hear, listen, and recognize the destruction before them as a judgment from the Lord Himself. It's a warning, a desperate cry for repentance. The climax comes especially in verse 7:

> Like warriors they charge;
> like soldiers they scale the wall.
> They march each on his way;
> they do not swerve from their paths.

It's an army approaching. Their strength is so great, Joel says, that even (2:10) "the earth quakes before them; the heavens tremble." There are cosmic reverberations on account of this judgment. And it's here, right before them. Surrounded by the army of death—in fact, right in the midst of it all—Joel puts the words of despair right into their mouths: "who can endure it?" (2:11).

2 "Yet Even Now" (Joel 2:12–13)

And then one little word changes the whole tenor of this prophecy: "Yet" (2:12). It's as if total annihilation was staved off by a single utterance: "Yet even now." Now—as the city is as good as captured, as the citizens are as good as slaves—even now is the time of repentance. Even at the end, even in the end, the call to repent stands: (2:12) "Return to Me with all your heart, with fasting, with weeping, and with mourning."

It's not too late. On the last breath, at the last moment, when all is gone and sure devastation is at hand, repent. Confess and believe. Turn from self-trust and cling to Christ alone. It's not too late. As Joel says, (2:13) "rend your hearts and not your garments." When your back is to the wall, there's no time to play the game of piecemeal repentance—there's no holding back. All you have must be laid bare before God. When the end is near, there's no sense in giving some to God and holding on to the rest for yourself. God doesn't want to forgive just some or part, He wants to have mercy on all. And that means you, all of you, the whole you. So, "return to the Lord your God."

But why? What good is this sort of God? What is He like? Who is He? Joel proclaims God as He has revealed Himself in the witness of Moses: (2:13) "For He is gracious and merciful, slow to anger, and abounding in steadfast love." These are the attributes of God. It's what God is like, who He is. Therefore, precisely because this God is the God of mercy, there is a "yet even now." He is the God who forgives completely and wholly and repeatedly. He forgives without and before our merit and worthiness. He forgives without condition or favoritism. That's just who He is. With this God, steadfast love abounds. It knows no limits. It never ceases. It's never quenched. And this love of God is seen and known and made certain for us in the cross of Christ. That is the turning point. That is the climax. It's there—on the cross—that we have our "yet even now."

3 God Repents? (Joel 2:13–14)

The event of the cross is how we know God's love, because it's there that disaster does not come to you but to Christ. There, God turns His judgment from you to His Son. There, God repents. What? Really? God repents? Can you really say that? Joel did. Compare a couple translations of Joel 2:13b–14 (emphasis added):

> KJV:
> For He is gracious and merciful, slow to anger, and of great kindness, and *repenteth* Him of the evil.
> Who knoweth if He will return and *repent*, and leave a blessing behind Him; even a meat offering and a drink offering unto the Lord your God?
>
> ESV:
> For He is gracious and merciful,
> slow to anger, and abounding in steadfast love;
> and He *relents* over disaster.
> Who knows whether He will not turn and *relent*,
> and leave a blessing behind Him,
> a grain offering and a drink offering
> for the Lord your God?

God repents (turns from, changes His mind) about the judgment He intends whenever a prophet makes intercession. We'll see this especially in Amos 7, but it's found throughout the prophets. For example, God allows for His repentance over Sodom and Gomorrah as long as Abraham intercedes. The same goes for Moses: as long as he prays for the people, the Lord does not destroy them, despite their sin. The Lord notably tells Jeremiah three times *not* to intercede so that God could send His judgment. This is standard fare for the prophets: God repents of causing disaster or evil or judgment when His spokesman pleads with Him.

This is Joel's task. He first pleads with Israel to repent, to turn and believe. Then he draws them into who God is for them: (2:14 KJV) "Who knoweth if He will return and repent?" This same dialogue goes on in Jonah's book of prophecy as well: (3:9 KJV) "Who can tell if God will turn and repent, and turn away from His fierce anger, that we perish not?"

That God would change, or repent, seems foreign to us—even wrong, or blasphemous. But is this not the greatest sign of God's mercy—that He would turn from His anger and forgive? Reed Lessing notes in his commentary on Jonah, "It is not God Himself, His nature, His attributes, or His will that changes. Rather, God's *disposition* toward us changes so that we are no longer objects of His wrath but recipients of His love in Christ" (R. Reed Lessing, *Jonah* [St. Louis: CPH, 2007], 325).

The cross of Christ is the sign of God's ultimate repentance—the final change of His disposition toward us. There God changed His mind; there God turned from the evil He was about to do to us and all creation, and instead set forth His full wrath against His Son, Jesus. Christ is the true prophet: He lives to make intercession for us always before the heavenly throne (Hebrews 7:25). And thanks be to God for that! For it is by His constant intercession that we live and move and have our being.

4 Priestly Intercession (Joel 2:17–27)

Jesus Christ is not only the fulfillment of all the prophets but He is also the great High Priest. He offers sacrifice to atone for our sin; and His sacrifice is His own body and blood, shed once and for all for the sins of the whole world (Hebrews 9:26). In this self-sacrifice, God the Son stood between the altar and the vestibule, weeping and interceding for us. The event of the cross is our Lord Jesus saying to the Father, (Joel 2:17) "Spare Your people, O Lord, and make not Your heritage a reproach, a byword among the nations."

The priests that did this in Joel's prophecy are those priests who stand in the stead and by the command of Christ for the sake of the people of God. These priests are advocates with the Father, pleading for a different verdict, for mercy.

This priestly and prophetic intercession is not just for show. Prayer actually works; God works through prayer so that it actually does something. This is true not just for the Old Testament priests and prophets who lived many centuries before us but for us as well. We Christians are "a royal priesthood" (1 Peter 2:9). Being baptized into Christ Jesus, we are priests—able and even commanded to intercede with God in prayer. God promises to hear and listen and even have mercy. In fact, that's precisely what all intercessory prayer is: begging God to change His mind, to repent. It is also then trusting God to do what He has promised to do. It is trusting Him to hear our prayer, answer our prayer, and be gracious and merciful to us. Prayer asks God to be who He is *for us*. Luther teaches us in the Small Catechism, "But we pray in this petition that it may be done among us also" (Third Petition). And St. Bernard of Clairvaux once said, "God will give you whatever you ask for in prayer, or better."

Intercessory prayer doesn't change who God is, but it does change who God is for us. It petitions God to deal with us not in His wrath but with His mercy; not according to His justice, but according to His compassion. And the change in how He deals with us isn't based on our merit or worthiness, our honor or prestige, or anything in us—but solely on who He is. So it is that intercessory prayer must flow from faith. Faith alone trusts God to be who He has promised to be, even for us.

To those who believe that God could be who He is, even for the sinner, God does exactly that! Joel exclaims, (2:18–19)

> Then the LORD became jealous for His land
> and had pity on His people.
> The LORD answered and said to His people,
> "Behold, I am sending to you
> grain, wine, and oil,
> and you will be satisfied;
> and I will no more make you
> a reproach among the nations."

This is followed by a series of promises, a series of blessings, a series of great reversals! That's who God is! He is the God of great reversals, the God who doesn't give to us as we deserve. This God hears and answers prayer and then responds by giving Himself completely to the one in need. He removes the fear of punishment and death, and He creates peace and joy instead. (2:23) "Be glad," Joel shouts! "Rejoice in the LORD your God."

Joy always follows faith. The two go hand in hand. Joy isn't merely an emotion or a nice sentiment; it's the full-bodied trust that God will be who God will be for me. As joy flows from faith, faith flows from promise. The promise creates the faith. So it is that Joel creates faith in his hearers; he preaches the promises of God: (2:25–27)

> I will restore to you the years. . . .
> You shall eat in plenty and be satisfied,
> and praise the name of the LORD your God,
> who has dealt wondrously with you.
> And My people shall never again be put to shame. . . .
> I am the LORD your God and there is none else.

5 An Old Testament Pentecost (Joel 2:28–32)

Now comes a promise unlike the other promises. Some of these promises Joel mentions are fulfilled, at least in part, in Old Testament times. The land from time to time was left at ease and gave forth great fruit. The Lord truly was their God who was with them where He promised to be for them. But Joel now introduces a new promise, an end-times promise, a Pentecost promise: (2:28–32)

> And it shall come to pass afterward,
> that I will pour out My Spirit on all flesh;
> your sons and your daughters shall prophesy,
> your old men shall dream dreams,
> and your young men shall see visions.
> Even on the male and female servants
> in those days I will pour out My Spirit.
>
> And I will show wonders in the heavens and on the earth, blood and fire and columns of smoke. The sun shall be turned to darkness, and the moon to blood, before the great and awesome day of the LORD comes. And it shall come to pass that everyone who calls on the name of the LORD shall be saved. For in Mount Zion and in Jerusalem there shall be those who escape, as the LORD has said, and among the survivors shall be those whom the LORD calls.

That's quite a promise. But when is it fulfilled? Peter stands up with the eleven other apostles at Pentecost and declares its fulfillment at the third hour of the day (Acts 2:14–21). It wasn't drunkenness, as some supposed; it was the pouring out of the Spirit! It was the answer to Jesus' prayer in John 14:16–17: "I will ask the Father, and He will give you another Helper [another paraclete, advocate, intercessor!], to be with you forever, even the Spirit of truth." Pentecost is the Lord's great gift of the Spirit. It's also the fulfillment of Joel's prophecy, for by the Spirit, men can call upon God and be saved.

6 Oracles against the Nations (Joel 3)

Joel locates this promised Pentecost "in those days" (3:1). "Those days," or "at that time," is a way of speaking eschatologically—toward the end times. That's how the prophets and the Scriptures as a whole speak of the end, the last days. It is, again, "Day of the Lord" talk. That day, as we've mentioned before, is a day of wrath and a day of blessing. Joel is quite clear on this: (3:1–2) "In those days and at that time, when I restore the fortunes of Judah and Jerusalem, I will gather all the nations and bring them down to the Valley of Jehoshaphat. And I will enter into judgment with them there."

It's a day of salvation to the Lord's people who suffered. It's a day of condemnation to the nations under whom they suffered. The nations that reject this Lord are now the recipients of His wrath.

Joel 3 presents a regular formula found within the prophets called the Oracles against the Nations. We'll find this also when we get to Amos (1:3–2:16), but it also appears in much larger forms in Isaiah (13–23), Jeremiah (46–51), and Ezekiel (25–32). Typically, these Oracles against the Nations are words of judgment (Law) on foreign kingdoms and powers; but they are also words of peace and forgiveness (Gospel) for Judah or Israel as God's elect people being rescued from the fear of their enemies.

The battle scene depicted in these oracles calls to mind the Church Militant; that is, the Church in this present life in its struggle against its spiritual enemies: the world, our own sinful flesh, and the devil. Joel calls this Church to arms: (3:9–10) "Consecrate for war; stir up the mighty men. Let all the men of war draw near; let them come up. Beat your plowshares into swords, and your pruning hooks into spears; let the weak say, 'I am a warrior.'"

The image here of plowshares beaten into swords is a direct reversal of Isaiah and Micah (also set within a Last Day event): (Isaiah 2:4; see also Micah 4:3)

> He shall judge between the nations,
> and shall decide disputes for many peoples;
> and they shall beat their swords into plowshares,
> and their spears into pruning hooks;
> nation shall not lift up sword against nation,
> neither shall they learn war anymore.

While Micah and Isaiah give us a beautiful and serene picture of the Church Triumphant (i.e., the Church delivered from these troubles when Christ returns), Joel focuses on the Church Militant. But in order that we don't think of these two as separate churches—for we all confess in the creeds "I believe in *one* holy Christian and apostolic Church"—we must recognize that on the Last Day, the two sides come together. The Church Militant gives way to the Church Triumphant. The great battle that overthrows the nations finally delivers peace.

Joel then sets this day within the context of a harvest: (3:13) "Put in the sickle, for the harvest is ripe." That's the call of Christ as well! All is done, all is ready; the earth has produced automatically in response to the Word (Mark 4:28–29)—harvest the crop! Bring in the wheat, press the vine. It's all bread and wine, body and blood, death and life—it's all the cross.

Conclusion

As a prophet, Joel is given to peer into the heavenly council. There he sees in shadow what would be fulfilled in reality on the cross. So he says, (3:15) "The sun and the moon are darkened, and the stars withdraw their shining." Jesus roughly quotes this in speaking of the Last Day also, (Mark 13:24–25) "But in those days, after that tribulation, the sun will be darkened, and the moon will not give its light, and the stars will be falling from heaven, and the powers in the heavens will be shaken." Mark goes on to proclaim its fulfillment on the cross: (15:33) "And when the sixth hour had come, there was darkness over the whole land until the ninth hour."

The event of the cross is the fulfillment of these prophesies of the Last Day. The paradox of who God is and who man is meets on that cross. That is the harvest, that the war, that the roar from Zion (Joel 3:16). The judgment has been rendered; peace with God is restored. Now we with faith in Jesus just wait for the final consummation of that peace when our Lord Christ returns in glory. But even with the war and the battle—even with the Church Militant—Joel knows the final end is one of glory and peace; better yet, the end is a feast! (3:18) "The mountains shall drip sweet wine, and the hills shall flow with milk." The enemy will lie defeated once and for all. Blood will be avenged. And it's all Christ for you!

Concluding Activities

Conclude the session with an appropriate prayer and distribute the study leaflet for week 7.

From the Nations to Israel—Judgment for All!

Amos 1–2

Preparing for the Session

Central Focus

When the Lord speaks, He speaks to all. None is left out from judgment or blessing. This Word that comes to all mankind is the roar of the Lion of Judah—most loudly and clearly heard in the whispers that came from the cross of Christ.

Objectives

That participants, led by the Holy Spirit working through God's Word, will

1. become familiar with who Amos was and the context in which he preached;
2. associate the word of Amos with the Law/Gospel proclamation of Christ; and
3. discern the all-inclusive character of God's actions toward mankind, reflecting on what that means for each of them in their Christian life.

Note for the small-group leaders: Lesson notes and other materials you will need begin on page 68.

For the Lecture Leader

Session Plan

Worship

Begin the session with the hymn printed in the study leaflet. Accompaniments are available in denominational hymnals, such as *Lutheran Service Book* or *Lutheran Worship* (refer to hymnal index). (Note: Concordia Publishing House has available *The Concordia Organist*. All the initial worship hymns in the LifeLight courses are included in this resource. It's especially helpful for mission congregations and small parishes. See the list of study resources on page 7.) Follow with this prayer:

Prayer

O voice that shakes the wilderness and sends the creatures into labor (Psalm 29), as You send forth Your Word in time, first by the mouth of the prophet, then by the Word made flesh, and now in the proclamation of the Gospel of Jesus Christ, shake also our wilderness of sin, drawing us to repentance and to see Your grace in the eternal Word begotten of You. Through Jesus Christ, Your Son, our Lord, who lives and reigns with You and the Holy Spirit, one God now and forever. Amen.

Lecture Presentation

1 Amos: Who? What? Where? When? Why? (Amos 1:1)

Names mean something. This is true particularly in the Old Testament, but it's also evident in the New: (Matthew 1:21) "She will bear a son, and you shall call His name Jesus, for He will save His people from their sins." Jonah's name, meaning "dove," resembles his flightiness with regard to the call of the Lord. Jacob is the famous heel-grabber, the second in the womb to be the one who God chose to be greater than Esau. Abram becomes Abraham as the promise comes for him to be the "father of a multitude of nations" (Genesis 17:5). Amos, too, has a name that preaches, a name that means something bigger than just a title. That's how names work in the Scripture—they're taken up into the prophetic task and speak even when the prophet doesn't. The name Amos comes from the same root for weight, or burden, or something carried painstakingly. It's related to the "burden of the word of the Lord" in Zechariah 9:1; 12:1. Amos is a "burden."

The Word that Amos bears is certainly a burden, a weight—not only for him to carry as a faithful preacher and prophet of God but also to those who hear and must receive this Word. Luther even says of Amos, "He can well be called Amos, that is, 'a burden,' one who is hard to get along with and irritating" (AE 35:320). Whether or not he was a particularly irritating prophet, to be on the receiving end of his word—God's Word—is certainly burdensome! Amos calls a spade a spade—or better yet, a sin a sin. He holds kings and priests accountable. He calls out the wealthy for their neglect. He stands up for the little and weaker brother.

As we steadily make our way through this Book of the Twelve, we will get to know better the burdensome prophet, Amos—sometimes called "the prophet of doom." This designation will make much more sense as we wade our way through this series of prophecies. But we will also find that doom is certainly not the final word! And with that, we'll find the burden lifted.

Amos was a shepherd from Tekoa (1:1) and a tender of sycamore fig trees (7:14). Tekoa was a town about twelve miles south of Jerusalem, which means Amos came from the Southern Kingdom. However, Amos prophesied in the Northern Kingdom, "concerning Israel," alongside Hosea in the first half of the eighth century BC during the reigns of Uzziah down south and Jeroboam up north. Because Amos lists fewer kings than Hosea, many believe Amos to actually be the first of the writing prophets. We're able to date his prophecy fairly accurately because it locates the preaching "two years before the earthquake" (1:1). Archaeologists date this quake right around 760 BC, which snugly fits within the reigns of Uzziah and Jeroboam. The earthquake became a landmark in the timeline of eighth-century BC history—so much so that even Zechariah mentions it centuries later (14:5).

But more than a mere chronological landmark, this earthquake bears great theological significance. On the one hand, it serves as a sign to validate the prophecy of Amos as the Word of the Lord to those who felt its shocks under their feet, especially the prophecy of 9:1: "Strike the capitals until the thresholds shake, and shatter them on the heads of all the people."

On the other hand, the much greater fulfillment of that prophecy takes place when the ground shakes under the cross as Jesus took His last breath (Matthew 27:51–53). And then another earthquake signals the resurrection of this Eternal Word (Matthew 28:2). Lastly, perhaps as a final aftershock, the reverberations of this great earthquake that occurred at the cross and at the tomb, will be felt on the Last Day when Christ returns in judgment (Matthew 24:29). Indeed, every quake of the earth today calls our hearts and minds to the promise of the Last Day and the judgment rendered already for us on the cross.

Now, it goes without saying, but Amos was a prophet. Not only is his pastoral preaching and writing located within the Book of the Twelve Prophets but also all the characteristics of prophecy are present in this work. Notably, it's all rooted in the words of Amos 1:1: "The words of Amos . . . which he saw." We'll discuss his standing as prophet in further detail when we come to his exchange with the priest Amaziah. For now, we're told that Amos saw the words and subsequently spoke the words. That's what prophets do: see and proclaim. A prophet is nothing more than the delivery point of the Lord's Word, His mouthpiece into the world.

2 Lion of the Tribe of Judah (Amos 1:2)

So what does this Amos proclaim? The first thing off his lips is the lion's roar (1:2). Here we recall Joel and see how nicely these two books of prophecy have been stitched together. Joel preaches, (3:16) "The Lord roars from Zion, and utters His voice from Jerusalem." Hosea said similarly, (11:10) "They shall go after the Lord; He will roar like a lion; when He roars, His children shall come trembling . . . like birds from Egypt." But what is this lion's roar?

One does not need to meet a lion face-to-face in the wild to know well enough that the roar of a lion paralyzes his target. This territorial roar comes before the attack, as a warning. Our Lord's paralyzing Word of the Law also roars from Zion. From the temple in Jerusalem is where this Word goes forth, calling sinners to repentance—a warning before the destruction.

Absolutely vital to understanding Amos, though, is recognizing the emphasis on Zion and Jerusalem. It is clearly the Lord's Word that does the roaring—not something Amos makes up on his own. And this Word of the Lord comes only out of His temple, His dwelling place (1 Kings 8:11). But the temple is located down south, in Jerusalem, the capital of the Southern Kingdom. Solomon's temple is the place where the Lord dwells and can be found by His people. There He locates Himself to bless and hear the prayers of His faithful, as well as to speak the Word of forgiveness. Amos, then, calls those in the north to come back to Jerusalem, back to the temple. The greatest offense among the people is not their manifold wickedness but their false worship.

Under Jeroboam, shrines in the north were established to conduct worship in the northern territories. This established political boundaries and ensured his kingdom a place to worship. That sounds great, economic, feasible, and practical—but there's one problem: that's not where the Lord promised to dwell! He promised to be located in the Jerusalem temple, not in Bethel or Gilgal! What this says, furthermore, is that Bethel and

Gilgal are silent. The Word roars so loudly and powerfully from Zion that it shows these other falsely established high places as mute. From them, our Lord does not speak—only from Jerusalem does the voice of the Lord ring forth.

This lion roar from Zion is a clear type, or picture, of Christ Jesus. In Christ, Paul says, (Colossians 2:9) "the whole fullness of deity dwells bodily." Therefore, we could say that, in Christ, God locates Himself for us. At Christmas, that means God was located in the lowliness of the manger or in the arms of mother Mary. On Maundy Thursday, God located Himself in the upper room and then in the bread and wine. On Good Friday, God located Himself on the cross—there He bound Himself to the wood, to be seen and found by all who lifted their eyes. And on Easter Sunday, our Lord and God located Himself out of the tomb; along the Emmaus Road; by the sea, catching fish; and, as Paul says, appearing to more than five hundred people (1 Corinthians 15:6). In the flesh and blood of Jesus, God Himself roars. Out of the mouth of Christ flows the Word, the warning call to repentance as well as the blessing of life everlasting. Zion, Jerusalem, the temple are all foreshadows of the man Jesus. He is, as Revelation 5:5 tells us, the "Lion of the tribe of Judah."

3 More Oracles against the Nations (Amos 1:3–2:5)

We've mentioned that Amos was a southern prophet who traveled up north and preached in the Kingdom of Israel. But early in his book of prophecy, Amos lets it be known that his word—the Lord's Word—extends throughout the world. The Lord roars from Zion, but that roar is heard and strikes fear into those not only in the Northern Kingdom but also in the surrounding towns, cities, and regions. Chapters 1 and 2 make up what is often called "the Oracles against the Nations."

Amos isn't unique. Especially among the Book of the Twelve, the prophets address words of judgment to the surrounding nations. Obadiah addresses Edom, while Jonah begrudgingly preaches to Nineveh. Nahum continues with Nineveh, while Habakkuk addresses the Babylonians. Zephaniah judges the nations broadly, while Malachi proclaims that the Lord will be "great among the nations" (1:11). Isaiah, Jeremiah, and Ezekiel all compose large sections within their prophecy of such oracles as these in Amos (see Isaiah 13–23; Jeremiah 46–51; Ezekiel 25–32). They are words, proclamations, preachings of judgment against the enemy nations.

In his first two chapters, Amos renders judgment upon Damascus, Gaza, Tyre, Edom, Ammon, and Moab. Each of these locations receive the guilty verdict for various crimes committed against humanity, and consequently, against the Lord Himself. Damascus tortured Israelites, and Gaza captured people and exiled them, possibly as slaves, to Edom. Tyre failed to keep the covenant, and Edom tracked down Israel violently, showing no mercy. Ammon murdered pregnant women and their unborn children—a reprehensible crime! Moab burned the bones of Edom's king to lime, perhaps even using these limed bones in plaster for a building. Each nation desecrates some portion of time: desecrating the future through the murder of unborn children, desecrating the past by annihilating the king's body, and desecrating the present by failing to show mercy and keep the covenant grace.

Typically, the purpose of the Oracles against the Nations is to elicit hope and joy. Oddly enough, these words are intended largely as words of comfort, assurance, and salvation. For God to destroy the wicked nations is for Him to come to the aid and salvation of Israel, to free them from their bondage and the evil intended against them. Jeremiah says it this way: (46:27–28)

> But fear not, O Jacob My servant,
> nor be dismayed, O Israel,
> for behold, I will save you from far away,
> and your offspring from the land of their captivity.
> Jacob shall return and have quiet and ease,
> and none shall make him afraid.
> Fear not, O Jacob My servant,
> declares the LORD,
> for I am with you.
> I will make a full end of the nations
> to which I have driven you,
> but of you I will not make a full end.

These Oracles against the Nations were intended as pure Law to the heathen peoples but pure Gospel to the nation of Israel.

4 Not Seven but All

These oracles follow a standard formula as Amos presents them. It is always "for three . . . and for four" (1:3, 6, 9, 11, 13; 2:1, 4, 6). Now, simple math might suggest that 3 and 4 gives 7. This 7, as Scripture often speaks in terms of symbolically weighted numbers, denotes something beyond mere numbering. Seven is the number of completion. It encapsulates the entire week of creation, even the Sabbath rest. While the mark on Cain yielded a sevenfold vengeance (Genesis 4:15), seventy times seven is the total forgiveness we are to have for our neighbor (Matthew 18:21–22). Sometimes translated as "seventy-seven," this number also shows the undoing of the sin of Lamech (Genesis 4:24). Seven is perfect, total, complete, whole. Amos proclaims that the nations have reached their fullness of sin—they've stirred the Lord to action.

But not just seven, 3 + 4 speaks of an ongoing increase of sin. Is it three, or four, or more yet? That's how Amos understands this fullness of sin: ongoing, never-ending, unquenchable desire for more. This captures rightly the reality of our sin as well. We should not think of our sin merely in terms of the symptoms or actual sins we commit. In fact, it's much deeper than that. Our sin has so infected us that we rightly confess in the Divine Service that, "we are by nature sinful and unclean." We weren't created this way, but with Adam's fall we were all infested with this sinful plague. So our sin is also innumerable: (Psalm 19:12) "Who can discern his errors?" So it was for the nations.

This 3 + 4 is a standard formula that appears beyond Amos. The appendix to the Book of Proverbs (ch. 30) lists a series of 3 + 4 sayings (vv. 15, 18, 21, 29). Moses also speaks of "the third and the fourth generation" (Exodus 20:5; 34:7). This literary pattern also highlights the Lord's lengthy patience. When the fullness of time comes for the payment of sin, we see that Christ Himself takes the 3 + 4 upon Himself. There, on the cross, God (3) and man (4) come together in one. Together they lay in the tomb, resting on that great Sabbath (John 19:31). On that cross, Jesus truly paid for the sins of the whole world—and not merely the deeds of sin but also the sinful core. He bore the full weight, the complete wrath of God—He truly set Himself in the place of the nations for us!

5 Climax toward Israel (Amos 2:6–16)

While the Oracles against the Nations as a literary work are typically Gospel utterances, that's not how Amos uses them. The rhetorical device Amos employs is called "capturing with kindness" (*captatio benevolentiae*). What this means is that he captures his audience's attention by gathering them all on his side against the enemies—those people out there—and then, when they're most comfortable, he lets his allies have it: "the knockout blow" (see H. Hummel, *The Word Becoming Flesh* [St. Louis: CPH, 1979], 312). Amos doesn't stop with the foreign nations; he then includes Judah and Israel as well. And not only that but Israel gets it worse than anyone! Amos uses a Gospel-themed structure to preach some of the harshest Law they've heard.

So what's the point in these oracles? Precisely to shake Israel to its very core. While they would have listened along, nodding their heads, expecting to hear a word of hope and consolation for their nation, despite the sin of the enemies, Amos instead shows them their sin. It is a preaching of the Law. To what end? For their repentance. Israel's sin is against both the natural law, which the nations are also guilty of, and also the revealed Law of Sinai. They've rejected the Lord's Word as He has promised to give and locate it. This is especially evident in their false worship—for truly the worship reflects the faith. They worship in the wrong way at the wrong place because they believe wrongly about this God.

This fact is made painfully clear by the Lord's insistence that their livelihood was from Him and not another. We saw this plainly in Hosea as well, where, out of jealousy, the Lord pleads with Gomer, telling her it was He that loved and cared and protected and provided. So also here in Amos: (2:9–11)

> "Yet it was I who destroyed the Amorite before them,
> whose height was like the height of the cedars
> and who was as strong as the oaks;
> I destroyed his fruit above
> and his roots beneath.
> Also it was I who brought you up out of the land of Egypt
> and led you forty years in the wilderness,
> to possess the land of the Amorite.
> And I raised up some of your sons for prophets,
> and some of your young men for Nazirites.
> Is it not indeed so, O people of Israel?"
> declares the LORD.

Here the Lord indicts Israel for breaking the whole covenant. They've forgotten the Lord as giver and protector, seeking to find their security in themselves, in their wealth and prosperity. Israel ought to know better—and as we hear Amos's preaching today, we ought to know better too! We also must quit looking at the nations and the heathen and "that sinful world out there." We must recognize that the sin of the nations pales in comparison to the sin within our heart. And we are without excuse: both the Law inscribed on our conscience as well as the reality of the world around, together with the Law spoken from the pulpit week in and week out, all show us our sin and call us to repentance.

Conclusion: When God Is Your Enemy

What is the sinner to do with God as the enemy? That's the situation we find ourselves in as we hear this roar from Zion in Amos's preaching. We hear a full and heavy dosage of the Law of God. We're convicted of our many sins—sins against humanity and against divinity, sins against Christ. Like Judah, we have forgotten and rejected the teaching of the Word of the Lord, along with the practice thereof. We've run after lies, typically of our own devising, rather than hearing and keeping the Word spoken by the mouths of our pastors. Like Israel, we have joined Judas in selling the Righteous One, Jesus Christ, for silver (Amos 2:6; see Matthew 26:15). We have neglected the weakest among us, turning aside from the afflicted (Amos 2:7). Our worship and prayers have faltered as we run to any and all altars without recognizing how each speaks a different word about God. We delight in the convenient and the practical, avoiding any cross possible. When this is who you are, what do you do?

When God is your enemy, you pray for Him to change. We all deserve for God to be against us. But that's not who God is by nature. We've already run into this with Joel's prophecy. God is by nature "slow to anger, and abounding in steadfast love and faithfulness" (Exodus 34:6). God does not want any to perish, but for all to come to a knowledge of the truth (1 Timothy 2:4). In Christ, God longs to gather all His children under His wings (Matthew 23:37). And if this is who God is, then our prayer is that God would be who God has said He will be for us. Luther highlights this throughout his Small Catechism. In each petition of the Lord's Prayer, he notes that God does all these things even without our asking, "but we pray in this petition that it may be done among us also."

When God is your enemy, repent. Hear the word of the prophet, and justify God by saying, "Yes, Lord. I am as you say." That's confession. It recognizes the truth, even when the truth calls us enemies of God. But then, repentance includes also the faith, the trust that this God, who is our judge, will be who He has promised to be. We'll see throughout Amos that the Northern Kingdom has no desire for God to be as He has said. They'd rather have Him on their terms, in their high places, with their doctrine and practice. Such arrogance is evidence of a 3 + 4 sort of sinfulness. Only Christ can bear that sort of sin and yet not perish. Thanks be to God that Christ has truly heeded the prophetic word of His Father and obeyed all, even unto death, for us!

Concluding Activities

Conclude the session with an appropriate prayer and distribute the study leaflet for week 8.

The Lord and His People

Amos 3–6

Preparing for the Session

Central Focus

The Lord and His people are not "in a relationship" as social networks might phrase it today. As Hosea taught us, they are married—joined together by the blood of the Lamb. This covenantal union is repeatedly broken by the people of God; yet, it is also repeatedly restored by God Himself through His Word as revealed by the prophet.

Objectives

That participants, led by the Holy Spirit working through God's Word, will

1. critique Israel's unfaithfulness with their own repentant hearts;

2. understand the workings of a prophet in view of the heavenly council; and

3. analyze the name of God in light of His promised presence in and with that name, even among them in their baptismal grace.

Note for the small-group leaders: Lesson notes and other materials you will need begin on page 70.

For the Lecture Leader

Session Plan

Worship

Begin the session with the hymn printed in the study leaflet. Accompaniments are available in denominational hymnals, such as *Lutheran Service Book* or *Lutheran Worship* (refer to hymnal index). (Note: Concordia Publishing House has available *The Concordia Organist*. All the initial worship hymns in the LifeLight courses are included in this resource. It's especially helpful for mission congregations and small parishes. See the list of study resources on page 7.) Follow with this prayer:

Prayer

Woe, O Lord, to us who break the covenant of Your love! Do not hide Your gracious face from us in our distress, but reveal Your favor by the light of Your face. Shine upon us in mercy. Bestow Your name upon us in Your promise of life. Turn us from our sin, O Lord, and teach us to seek You and live! In the holy and precious name of Your only-begotten Son, Jesus Christ. Amen.

Lecture Presentation

1 Is God Angry for No Reason? (Amos 3:1–8)

One of the greatest frustrations is being furious at another person when he or she does not know why. This occurs frequently in marriage; perhaps a husband is dumbfounded at his wife's anger. It happens with children too: "Go sit in time-out and think about why you're in trouble!" As sinners, we often have a problem knowing what we did wrong. We are so focused on ourselves, on justifying ourselves, that we often think we're innocent. That's the way we are before God as well—horribly guilty, yet acting as if we're doing just fine.

Israel was the same way. Though they were the Lord's chosen people, His elect children, they deserted Him and thought they did no wrong. And then, when "the Lord roars from Zion" (Amos 1:2), they wonder why. "What's the big deal?" they ask. More pointedly to Amos, they ask, "Who are you to speak to us that way?" In answer to this, Amos asks seven rhetorical questions—each should properly be answered "No." (3:3–6)

> Do two walk together,
> unless they have agreed to meet?
> Does a lion roar in the forest,
> when he has no prey?
> Does a young lion cry out from his den,
> if he has taken nothing?
> Does a bird fall in a snare on the earth,
> when there is no trap for it?
> Does a snare spring up from the ground,
> when it has taken nothing?
> Is a trumpet blown in a city,
> and the people are not afraid?
> Does disaster come to a city,
> unless the Lord has done it?

Interestingly, Amos likens the Lord's Word of judgment to two people walking together in agreement. This has been variously interpreted, but it seems Luther is right on target:

> We apply the proverb this way: These two are God and His people. The Lord is saying, as it were: "You know from this that I am your adversary, that I am not standing at your side. In fact, we are not walking on the same road as we ought. I am not in agreement with you. Nevertheless, you want to escape unpunished. You are wicked and have transgressed the Law; yet you argue over your innocence. Therefore, because I am just, I will not spare your unrighteousness. I will not stop striking you until you agree with Me, which you now do not, for you are following a road that goes away from Me." (*AE* 18:145).

Israel and the Lord agreed to meet at Sinai. There a covenant was established; there the people gave full assent: (Exodus 24:7–8)

> Then [Moses] took the Book of the Covenant and read it in the hearing of the people. And they said, "All that the Lord has spoken we will do, and we will be obedient." And Moses took the blood and threw it on the people and said, "Behold the blood of the covenant that the Lord has made with you in accordance with all these words."

The two walked together (the Lord and His people) because they agreed to meet. But now, they don't. Now, they walk separately. Now, Israel has gone her way and the Lord responds justly. But Israel is in denial: both of the Lord and His prophet.

The next rhetorical question calls to mind again the Lord's roar. Does He utter His voice from Zion without purpose? Does the Lord rebuke Israel flippantly? Has He just had a bad day, or little sleep, or is He actually angry with someone else? No. The Lord roars because He has prey—the people of Israel! He is the young lion crying out from His den because He has His adversary within His paws. He has caught the flighty bird in His trap, He has sprung from the ground, He has blown the trumpet, He has terrified His enemy. And then, most climactically of all, the Lord has brought disaster to the city; He has caused them this evil they face. The Lord has done it.

But can God bring evil? What does this mean? The word used for "disaster" (Amos 3:6) could also be translated "evil." Amos makes it very clear that, indeed, the Lord has done this disaster in Israel. He has executed His judgment—and He was right to do it. Other prophets have spoken similarly: (Isaiah 45:7) "I form light and create darkness, I make well-being and create calamity [evil], I am the Lord, who does all these things." The evil being done is the evil of judgment. It's the just penalty for sin. Ultimately, the evil/disaster that God sends is the cross. There we see the greatest picture of our God sending evil—but that is also the greatest image of mercy. There evil is once and for all removed from us. There the roar of the lion has gone out most loud and clear—and yet not against us; we were not in the paws of God, but His Son was!

2 The Council of God (Amos 3:7)

This is the message of Amos—hidden in time, but revealed fully on the cross. And seeing such a Word, "Who can but prophecy?" (Amos 3:8). Amos brings the word that God is angry—but it's certainly full of purpose. His anger is just and true and rightly leveled against the sin of Israel. But this wrath will not come apart from the word of the prophet; (3:7) "For the Lord God does nothing without revealing His secret to His servants the prophets."

Amos teaches us a bit about how the prophets work. The prophet always experiences the Word of God as conversation and a vision, located in what the Scriptures call the heavenly council (Psalm 82:1; 89:7). First and foremost, the council is the place where the Lord delivers His Word. It's truly a revelation. The divine council includes angels, archangels, and all the company of heaven; and with them, the Lord invites His prophets too. So the council is the location of the Lord, and His Word, and therefore also the prophets—all in conversation together. The Lord speaks and His Word takes shape—that's why the prophets see visions and are first called "seers" (1 Samuel 9:9).

By inviting His prophets to see and hear the vision of His Word, the Lord sends them to go and speak forth this Word. So we rightly speak of prophets as forth-tellers. We go wrong when we picture the prophets primarily as fore-tellers, or predictors of the future. Prophets do so only at God's direction. There's nothing within them that allows them to predict or foresee the future. Rather, by their standing within the heavenly council, the vision they see may be in our understanding past, present, or future. They simply see the reality and speak it forth. So everything our Lord does, He first reveals to His servants the prophets (Amos 3:7).

3 The Wealth of the Nation (Amos 3:12–15)

What is this Word revealed to Amos? It's a word of judgment, for sure, but also a word of promise. Throughout the Prophets, there is a constant theme of the remnant: (Isaiah 10:20–22)

> In that day the remnant of Israel and the survivors of the house of Jacob will no more lean on him who struck them, but will lean on the LORD, the Holy One of Israel, in truth. A remnant will return, the remnant of Jacob, to the mighty God. For though your people Israel be as the sand of the sea, only a remnant of them will return. Destruction is decreed, overflowing with righteousness.

This remnant, on the one hand, suggests a great destruction—so much so that the majority are destroyed. And yet, the remnant also speaks of our Lord's mercy, wherein some are saved—albeit only a few. Jesus carries on this theme when He says, (Matthew 7:13–14) "Enter by the narrow gate. For the gate is wide and the way is easy that leads to destruction, and those who enter by it are many. For the gate is narrow and the way is hard that leads to life, and those who find it are few." It's this few, this remnant, that Amos speaks of: (3:12) "As the shepherd rescues from the mouth of the lion two legs, or a piece of an ear, so shall the people of Israel who dwell in Samaria be rescued, with the corner of a couch and a part of a bed." But why?

Amos unveils Israel's manifold sin throughout his prophecy, but one thing shines particularly brightly: Israel's idolatry. This idolatry, witnessed most clearly at the "altars of Bethel" (3:14), spawns forth into pride and greed, covetousness, and all sorts of deception. In this Northern Kingdom particularly, the love of money seems to be the true root of all their evils. So our Lord's Word of wrath comes in the form of destroying their wealth—or as John the Baptist would be sent to proclaim: (Luke 3:5) "Every mountain and hill shall be made low." The wealth of the nation has been Israel's downfall, a steady pace headlong toward pure idolatry.

4 Yet You Did Not Repent (Amos 4:1–12)

This wealth led to gluttony. Amos even calls them "cows" (4:1), who "oppress the poor" and "crush the needy" and who never get enough to drink. But for all Israel's wealth, it wasn't simply riches that brought the Lord's judgment. It was idolatry. It was that they had "abandoned the love [they] had at first" (Revelation 2:4), and committed the adultery Hosea so well described.

Israel's idolatry manifests itself most fully at the high places of Bethel and Gilgal. We came across these already with Hosea (4:15). Amos taunts Israel for her utter faithfulness to these false worship practices: (4:4–5)

> Come to Bethel, and transgress;
> to Gilgal, and multiply transgression;
> bring your sacrifices every morning,
> your tithes every three days;
> offer a sacrifice of thanksgiving of that which is leavened,
> and proclaim free will offerings, publish them;
> for so you love to do, O people of Israel!

It's disturbing how much we are like Israel in this respect: we offer much greater devotion to our idols and pet sins than we do to our Lord! Consider the time and devotion we give to checking Facebook status updates or following Twitter feeds. What if we gave equal time to the study of God's Word—let alone more time?

What is the Lord to do with Israel's blatant devotion to false gods? How can the Lord stand to be set on a par with Baal and the horrendous practices associated with him? The Lord brings punishments and disciplines with the hope to train His people and draw them back to Himself. First it's famine and then it's drought—"yet you did not return to Me" (Amos 4:6b, 8b). Then He destroys the crops and sends forth pestilence and sword and an army of destruction—"yet you did not return to me" (4:9b, 10b, 11b). And then comes the finale: (4:12) "Therefore thus I will do to you, O Israel . . . prepare to meet your God, O Israel!"

There's nothing more fearful than meeting God face-to-face in your sin—nothing more terrifying, nothing more deadly. We've largely forgotten this side of who God is: "a consuming fire" (Deuteronomy 4:24). Today's culture thinks it has managed to tame God. We perceive Him as nice and manageable. That's part of what makes Amos such a needed prophet today: he calls us to hear the Lion's roar. A delightful picture of this imagery is given to us in C. S. Lewis's *Chronicles of Narnia: The Lion, the Witch, and the Wardrobe*. Young Lucy asks Mr. Beaver if Aslan, the lion character, is safe to be around. Mr. Beaver replies that Aslan is not safe—but he is good. That's a remarkably good illustration of the Lord God Himself. For the sinner, He's certainly *not* safe. But He's good.

And in His goodness, in His desire for man, God does what it takes to bring repentance. Whether disaster or calamity or evil—whatever you choose to call it—the Lord brings these about not for fun or sadistic pleasure but for the sake of repentance. He does it in order to present again before Israel His grace. The theologians speak of God's two wills: an antecedent, or cursory, will, and His ultimate, fulfilled will. The first is the Law, the second the Gospel. The first is His judgment, the second, His grace. His anger isn't primary to who He is, but it's a consequence of the fall. As such, the anger of the Lord—His *roar*—strikes in order to bring about His joy, pleasure, grace, and forgiveness. All He does is done in love for the sinner.

5 Hymns and a Name (Amos 4:13; 5:8–9)

So that we don't forget this love of God, Amos breaks into song. Twice in chapters 4–5, Amos's poetry changes tunes and he sings the glory of the Lord: (4:13)

> For behold, He who forms the mountains and creates the wind,
> and declares to man what is his thought,
> who makes the morning darkness,
> and treads on the heights of the earth—
> the LORD, the God of hosts, is His name!

God is the Creator, the Mind, the Glory of heaven and earth. So when He commands creation as He does, He does it for the glory of His people. But notice the emphasis on the name. Again, in the second hymn, Amos sings: (5:8b) "The LORD is His name." What's in the name? Well, in a word, everything. The name of the Lord is the point and access of blessing. That's how God gave Himself to His people—always with the name. See, for example, in Exodus: (3:13–14) "Then Moses said to God, 'If I come to the people of Israel and say to them, "The God of your fathers has sent me to you," and they ask me, "What is His name?" what shall I say to them?' God said to Moses, 'I AM WHO I AM.' And He said, 'Say this to the people of Israel, "I AM has sent me to you."'"

Moses again gets the name of God while hidden in the cleft of the rock: (Exodus 34:5–7)

> The LORD descended in the cloud and stood with him there, and proclaimed the name of the LORD. The LORD passed before him and proclaimed, "The LORD, the LORD, a God merciful and gracious, slow to anger, and abounding in steadfast love and faithfulness, keeping steadfast love for thousands, forgiving iniquity and transgression and sin, but who will by no means clear the guilty, visiting the iniquity of the fathers on the children and on the children's children, to the third and the fourth generation."

This name is given to the people in the priestly blessing: (Numbers 6:24–27)

> The LORD bless you and keep you;
> the LORD make His face to shine upon you
> and be gracious to you;
> the LORD lift up His countenance upon you
> and give you peace.
> So shall they put My name upon the people of Israel,
> and I will bless them.

Then, climactically for Israel, God causes His name to dwell with men on earth: (1 Kings 9:3) "I have heard your prayer and your plea, which you have made before Me. I have consecrated this house that you have built, by putting My name there forever." It's all in the name: the presence, the power, the access, the grace. God is with His people wherever His name is. That's why Amos sings of the name—for He sings of the Lord and His glory and His presence among His people.

6 Woe! (Amos 5:16–6:14)

But what of those who do not repent? What happens to those who hear this roar and think nothing of it? What about those who aren't woken from their complacency, who don't see their sin, who have no desire for repentance? What of those who have no fear of the Lord and who "desire the day of the LORD" (Amos 5:18)?

For such as these, there's only one word: "Woe!" (Amos 5:18; 6:1, 4). That day (which we've already spoken at length about) will not be as they expect. Amos describes it as an inescapable wrath: fleeing from a lion only to meet a bear, and escaping the bear to be stung with the poisonous and deadly bite of the serpent—just when he thought he was safe (Amos 5:19).

For those who don't "bear fruit in keeping with repentance" (Matthew 3:8), no offering will suffice. There will be no making up for lost time, no second chances, no do-overs. Once that day comes, there will be no mulligans, no matter how sincere the desire might be. As Amos says, (5:24) "Justice [will] roll down like waters." This will be cause of great joy and reprieve for those clinging to the name; but justice is never desired for those caught in their sin.

Those "at ease" (6:1) will be shaken. Those taking for granted their time of repentance will be sorely disappointed. For them, there will be exile, desertion, a separation from God. The New Testament calls this separation a place of "weeping and gnashing of teeth" (Matthew 13:50). No more feasts or festivals or revelry or joy for those who would have it their way. In fact, hell is the place where you finally and fully "have it your way." It's the culmination of pride, which the Lord abhors (Amos 6:8). It's a total separation from grace and from the love of God.

Woe to those who run in such a way, who close their ears and harden their hearts—both Israel of old and those today. Amos incites within us a passion also for the lost. He calls us to a godly sense of urgency, a pleading and begging for repentance. He draws us into a confession of our sin, showing forth our own pride and arrogance, our own comfort and "have-it-your-way attitude." He calls us to seek the Lord, the good, and live! But woe to those who will not! Christ says in His sadness, (Matthew 23:37) "O Jerusalem, Jerusalem, the city that kills the prophets and stones those who are sent to it! How often would I have gathered your children together as a hen gathers her brood under her wings, and you were not willing!" Our destruction is ultimately our fault.

Conclusion: Seek Me and Live (Amos 5:4–7, 10–15)

Now, because the Lord's name is what it is—(Exodus 34:6) "merciful and gracious, slow to anger, and abounding in steadfast love and faithfulness"—the Lord continues to plead for His people. Utter destruction is not His will. As our Lord says in Ezekiel (33:11), "I have no pleasure in the death of the wicked, but that the wicked turn from his way and live." The Lord loves His people and calls them to repent—to confess and believe.

Three times in chapter 5, Amos begs Israel with a similar phrase:

> (V. 4) Seek Me and live.
>
> (V. 6) Seek the Lord and live.
>
> (V. 14) Seek good, and not evil, that you may live.

That's how it is with our Lord. He's a jealous God (Deuteronomy 4:24). He won't share us: not with money or wealth or Baal or anything else. "Seek Me" He says, "But do not seek Bethel" (Amos 5:5). Don't seek evil or falsehood or lies or deceit or deception. Don't seek your death. Life is in God alone. In His name, all the blessings flow. Where He has promised to be for you—that's where you ought to be! This is the cry of Amos. You can hear the tremble in his tone, the pleading in his eyes: (Amos 5:15)

> Hate evil, and love good,
> and establish justice in the gate;
> it may be that the Lord, the God of hosts,
> will be gracious to the remnant of Joseph.

This "it may be" is the most profound "perhaps" of Scripture. It comes again in Jonah (3:9), and we've heard it already in Joel (2:14). Who knows? Despite all this wickedness, despite the many transgressions and the great sins (Amos 5:12), perhaps God will still be God for Israel.

That is the hope of faith. The hope we have as Christians trusts God to be God despite our sin—indeed, precisely in the face of our sin. We trust that He will be who He will be (the great "I am") for us—not because of anything in us but because of everything in Him. That's faith. That's seeking the Lord. That's what it means to cling to the name of God. And this is the call of repentance that Amos is ringing out for all to hear and for all to believe.

Concluding Activities

Conclude the session with an appropriate prayer and distribute the study leaflet for week 9.

The Prophetic Vision

Amos 7–9

Preparing for the Session

Central Focus

The true prophet stands before the face of God, sees and hears the Word God desires to impart, and then goes forth to speak this Word boldly to the Lord's own people. He speaks and does nothing of his own power or strength, but only that which comes from the Lord. And the true prophet delivers nothing else than Christ and Him crucified for us and for all!

Objectives

That participants, led by the Holy Spirit working through God's Word, will

1. comprehend the substance and structure of prophetic vision;
2. rejoice in prophetic intercession, especially the ever-present intercession of Christ on their behalf;
3. discern the fulfillment of all true prophets in the person and work of Jesus Christ; and
4. intercede in prayer for others.

Note for the small-group leaders: Lesson notes and other materials you will need begin on page 72.

For the Lecture Leader

Session Plan

Worship

Begin the session with the hymn printed in the study leaflet. Accompaniments are available in denominational hymnals, such as *Lutheran Service Book* or *Lutheran Worship* (refer to hymnal index). (Note: Concordia Publishing House has available *The Concordia Organist*. All the initial worship hymns in the LifeLight courses are included in this resource. It's especially helpful for mission congregations and small parishes. See the list of study resources on page 7.) Follow with this prayer:

Prayer

O Branch of Jesse and Key of David, Scepter of the House of Israel and risen Savior, enlighten our eyes with the light of Your presence among us. Speak forth Your Word into our ears and carry it down to our hearts and out of our hands, all for the works that You have set out in advance for us to walk in. In Your most holy name. Amen.

Lecture Presentation

1 The Prophet as Visionary (Amos 7:1)

We hear a lot today about having a vision. Every leadership manual or business seminar begins with a vision. Even some within the Church today are after vision statements and vision casting, all part of an effective leadership model. Vision speaks of a preferred future and a healthy sense of urgency about the direction and focus of the congregation. George Barna offers a number of working definitions of this vision in his book *The Power of Vision* (Ventura: Regal, 1992, 2003, 2009), where he emphasizes the desire to follow God's will.

This vision language, by and large, is not related to a concrete, tangible reality, something seen outside of us, but rather to thoughts, feelings, and desires that come from within. On the other hand, the vision language of Scripture is always located within what is called the divine or heavenly council (Psalm 82:1), which we spoke about in the last lesson. Most important here, the Word revealed in this council to the prophet is a real Word, an external Word, something that can be seen with the eye and heard with the ear.

And what happens if there is no vision? The Book of 1 Samuel gives us a starting point: (3:1) "The word of the LORD was rare in those days; there was no frequent vision." This lack of vision is not a good thing. As the narrative unfolds, Samuel is called to be Israel's prophet, their witness to the heavenly council. Another example is found in Proverbs, (29:18) "Where there is no prophetic vision the people cast off restraint." While this proverb is often taken out of context, it is talking precisely about the vision of the prophet within the heavenly council. Without a vision, there is fear, lawlessness, and recklessness. In Lamentations (2:9), Jeremiah cries out: "Her gates have sunk into the ground; he has ruined and broken her bars; her king and princes are among the nations; the law is no more, and her prophets find no vision from the LORD."

These prophetic visions are always from God, revealed in the heavenly council, and are never from man—no ecstatic experience or imaginative foresight or preferred future. You can't come up with a genuine vision from God, no matter who you are. But Israel had a way of doing just that: (Jeremiah 23:16) "Thus says the LORD of hosts: 'Do not listen to the words of the prophets who prophesy to you, filling you with vain hopes. They speak visions of their own minds, not from the mouth of the LORD.'"

This is what marks the false prophets: they have no vision—at least, no vision from the Lord. Their visions come from their own minds. So the Lord says, (Jeremiah 23:21–22)

> I did not send the prophets,
> yet they ran;
> I did not speak to them,
> yet they prophesied.
> But if they had stood in My council,
> then they would have proclaimed My words to My people,
> and they would have turned them from their evil way,
> and from the evil of their deeds.

Vision does not come from within us—our minds, our thoughts, our plans, our hopes. Vision comes from the Word of God alone. And that's how it is for Amos too.

So why stress about having these visions for the Church? Well, because that's what seems to work. But what are these visions? Where do they come from? And is this how the Church is given to speak? Or better, is that what Amos means when he relates a series of visions, saying, (7:1) "This is what the Lord GOD showed me"?

And this is the point: the visionary experience of the prophets, rooted in the revealed Word of the Lord and a true conversation with Him, will inform the Church's witness today and thereby firmly establish her mission in the concrete Word of God. That is, if you want a vision, you must seek the word of the prophet (Ezekiel 7:26), delivered now to us in Jesus Christ (Hebrews 1:1). And it is His revelatory Word that comes to us in the preaching of the Gospel and the administration of this Word made flesh in the Sacraments—if we've got a vision, it's Christ, the revealed Word and will of the Father for us.

2 Saying "No!" to God (Amos 7:1–6)

If prophetic vision is not some power or foresight within the prophet but an actual seeing and hearing of what our Lord communicates in the heavenly council, then the conversation at this council is of upmost importance both for Israel and for us. Central to this conversation is the prophet's "no."

One of the chief functions of a prophet is his appointment to speak back to the Lord, to argue his case (remember the "controversy," or *rîb,* of Hosea?). Perhaps the more comfortable language might be "to intercede for the people." When our Lord speaks His Word and presents His vision of justice to the prophet, there are times the prophet simply says, "No." Consider, for example, the experience of Amos (7:1–6). Twice, our Lord shows Amos a vision of destruction, and twice, Amos cries out against the vision: "O Lord GOD, please forgive! . . . O Lord GOD, please cease!" And twice, the Lord repents of the vision He showed to Amos.

Yes, I said, repent (see the KJV and our discussion in the previous lessons). Many recent English translations have piously scrubbed the strong Hebrew language that clearly presents our Lord repenting, changing His mind, turning from the evil He intended to do (see Isaiah 45:7 and Jeremiah 18:7–8). All of this turning and changing is tied to His interaction with His prophet.

This sort of intercession is precisely what Abraham, the first biblical figure called a prophet (Genesis 20:7), engaged in as he "stood before the LORD," pleading for Sodom (Genesis 18:22–33). More famous yet is the intercession of Moses, who stood in the breach between the Lord's wrath and the people of Israel (Exodus 32:11–14; Deuteronomy 9:13–19). Intercession was the primary practice of the prophets.

Prophets are the given intermediary between the Lord and His people Israel. The prophet is placed between God and man; and for man's sake, he both proclaims and intercedes (Jeremiah 18:20)—it's truly two-way communication. Through the office of the prophet, and notably through his intercessory prayer, the people have access to their God. Without prophetic intercession, the people are severed from the Lord. It's the prophet who brings both God and man together.

That's why the intercession of Amos is so important. Twice does God show visions of destruction, and twice Amos pleads for mercy. But after the third vision (Amos 7:7–9) there is no intercession. Why?

3 Amos and Amaziah: Not a Prophet, Not a Priest (Amos 7:10–17)

As the text of Amos unfolds, there's a sudden interruption. When chapter 7 began, there was a nice and comfortable formula: (1) "This is what the Lord God showed me"; (2) an account of the vision; (3) the interjection of the prophet—the prophetic "No"; and (4) the Lord repenting of the vision. This nice mixing of poetry and prose is rudely halted in 7:10 by the phrase "Then Amaziah . . ." Everything changes when Amaziah comes on the scene.

Who was Amaziah? He was a priest serving at Jeroboam's sanctuary at Bethel. Bethel was a town about 10 miles north of Jerusalem. It was home to one of the main sites of unauthorized worship in Israel. It was a shrine established by King Jeroboam and noted for its apostasy (see Hosea 4). Amaziah was the priest at this place of false worship and false doctrine together.

Amaziah, then, was no priest at all. Just because Jeroboam set him up as one; and just because he called himself a priest, perhaps even functioning as a priest in many ways; and just because the people who gathered together at Bethel called him "priest," that does not make him a priest of the one true God! God established His priesthood after the lineage of the Levites. Priests are called and made priests by God. Amaziah was a priest only by the command of Jeroboam, not of God. And Jeroboam, though he was king of the Northern Kingdom, did not have the divine authority to make such appointments. So at Bethel they were, in fact, playing church. Amaziah was not a priest.

The irony comes when Amaziah confronts Amos. He says, (Amos 7:12–13) "O seer, go, flee away to the land of Judah, and eat bread there, and prophesy there, but never again prophesy at Bethel, for it is the king's sanctuary, and it is a temple of the kingdom." As far as Amaziah is concerned, prophets come and go. They listen to the king and do as he says. Prophets get in line, obey the king's rules, and keep the statutes of his sanctuary and his temple.

To this sort of prophecy Amos replies: (7:14) "I was no prophet." But this simple statement that Amos wasn't a prophet does not reflect what he actually said in the original Hebrew. He literally says, "I am not a prophet." Why? Because he's not a prophet as Amaziah has just described what it means to be prophet. He doesn't and won't listen to the king's command. He doesn't pick and choose when to speak and when to keep quiet. Amos must say whatever the Lord tells him—no matter what. Amos is a true prophet who has stood in the Lord's council, heard His Word, seen His vision, and now comes to preach what the Lord declares. But a prophet of Bethel, Amos is not!

Amaziah is so used to being a priest of himself—that is, by his own desire and doing—that he puts that burden on Amos as well. He assumes Amos is also a prophet of himself, or of his own doing. But Amos boldly confesses that he is not a prophet of himself; of himself, he is a simple herdsman and tender of sycamore fig trees. Still, he is a prophet—not of himself but of God. As Amos says, (7:15) "The Lord took me from following the flock, and the Lord said to me . . ." In this way, the true prophet of God shows the ironic arrogance of the false priest of the king. And the words of judgment that follow fit the whole edifice created around this false worship and false doctrine together.

4 The End (Almost): Silence! (Amos 8)

The worship life in Bethel has so enraged the Lord that judgment must come forth. But this rage of the Lord, we'll see, is not the sort of pure anger we feel. We often lash out in judgment when we're angry, and we might do so uncontrollably. Our anger is never for the betterment of the other; it's always for their worse—that's why we hit harder than we were hit, or cut more deeply than the words cut into us. But our Lord, when He sends forth His anger, always sends it out in a controlled, justified, and measured way. It's not a reaction from the heat of passion but a calculated, just reward.

So the Lord shows Amos a final vision: a basket of summer fruit (8:1). Why? As a going-away present. The basket of summer fruit shows that the harvest has come—the fruits have ripened and already have been picked. Likely figs, the fruits in this basket are harvested in August and September, at the end of the season. And so the interpretation of this vision is an account of the end. The Lord says, (8:2–3)

> The end has come upon My people Israel;
> I will never again pass by them.
> The songs of the temple shall become wailings
> in that day.

The Lord goes on to describe the mass destruction. He speaks of bodies strewn about, the end of the temple song, and from the lips of all: "Silence!" (8:3). This "silence" was already heard back in 6:9–10:

> And if ten men remain in one house, they shall die.
> And when one's relative, the one who anoints him

> for burial, shall take him up to bring the bones out of the house, and shall say to him who is in the innermost parts of the house, "Is there still anyone with you?" he shall say, "No"; and he shall say, "Silence! We must not mention the name of the LORD."

Silence means an end to the prophet's intercession. Silence means an end to our Lord's word of grace. Silence means that all mouths have been stopped (Psalm 63:11). Silence is the mark of the end—the end of God's heavenly conversation with His people.

So when does this silence come? When will all of the world be hushed by the judgment of God? This again ties us well into our Day of the Lord, or the Last Day language so familiar to the Book of the Twelve. From our study of that day, we see that the world is hushed primarily on the cross. It's on the cross that the harvest is ripe and picked and set in a basket. It's on the cross of Christ that the temple song comes to an end and the wailings are heard throughout the land. On the cross, the bodies of all the dead are located within the lifeless corpse of Christ, the Son of God and the Son of man. On the cross, there's finally that silence. The sun closed its radiant mouth, casting darkness over the earth (Amos 8:9; Matthew 27:45). The curtain of the temple quieted its proclamation by rending in two. The earth itself let out a final groan at the great earthquake on that day, letting the land sit in silence as Christ, the very Word of God, hung silent on the cross.

If that's the silence Amos speaks of, then the basket of summer fruit handed to Israel is but an image or foreshadowing of the true Fruit of the Spirit hung from the cross. The destruction to come in the Northern Kingdom will pale in comparison to the crucifixion. The Assyrian invasion toward the end of the eighth century will simply be a foretaste of the cup of wrath that Christ our Lord drinks on the cross. And because of that, we know that the end is not yet.

5 A Famine of the Word (Amos 8:11–12)

That's the way Christians speak of the end days or the last things: as now and not yet. This works both for judgment and for blessing. In the midst of suffering, we're tied to our Lord's cross, experiencing His pain and agony, connected deeply with His sufferings for us. We feel that work of judgment now—recognizing all suffering as a glimpse of our own mortality—but we know that the end is not yet. On the other hand, our future joy in Christ is also ours now, even though we do not yet see its fullness.

But notice what those days bring: a famine of the Word. While a famine of food is certainly devastating in itself; that's a devastation only of the body. Jesus said, (Matthew 10:28) "Do not fear those who kill the body but cannot kill the soul. Rather fear Him who can destroy both soul and body in hell." That's what happens with a famine of the Word. It's a famine of God's favor, a famine of grace, a famine of prophetic intercession and divine counsel. Such a famine causes confusion and disarray: (Amos 8:12)

> They shall wander from sea to sea,
> and from north to east;
> they shall run to and fro, to seek the word of the LORD,
> but they shall not find it.

This famine of the Word is the worst judgment imaginable. It is a true hell. For the Word to be cut off from Israel is for God to be cut off from His people. Hell is precisely the separation from God. It's the separation from His goodness and grace, His mercy and compassion, His care and protection, and all that flows from Him. That is the Word for Israel from Amos's mouth. But it's not the final word!

Conclusion: A Risen David! (Amos 9:11–15)

The destruction that will surely take place in the Northern Kingdom at the false worship shrines of Bethel and Gilgal is not the end. Sure, it's the end for those bound to these places—but it's not an end to our Lord's love and care for Israel. He will not abandon His people. He will not desert His chosen and elect. He will not forsake Himself that marriage He entered into by His will. And so He again speaks words of promise.

Though somewhat rare in Amos's book of prophecy, the promise comes as a drink of cool water on a parched and thirsty land. It comes as sustenance for those starving for hope. And again, it's all located "in that day": (9:11)

> In that day I will raise up
> the booth of David that is fallen
> and repair its breaches,
> and raise up its ruins
> and rebuild it as in the days of old.

This is our Lord's resurrection talk coming from the mouth of His prophet Amos. It's all talk of Christ, the shoot of Jesse, the branch of David, the Son of God, and the Lion of Judah. He is the one who raises up the fallen and heals the brokenhearted. He is the one who restores all things in Himself—and not just mending the cracks, but bringing a full restoration: back to Eden and better! In this Christ, the remnant of Edom—that most heinous people—is forgiven. In Christ, the nations will seek the Lord, even those who "cast off all pity" (1:11) and "ripped open pregnant women in Gilead" (1:13). In the days of this Christ, and in His redemption, production of grain and grape will be doubled! Feasting and drinking will multiply! Joy and gladness, food and drink, wine and bread will be for all and always! That's the mark of this Christ: joy after joy.

What a joy to find here in Amos a word of joy connected to grain and wine (9:13). For what joy matches ours here on earth when we receive the grain and wine of the Sacrament of the Altar? What joy compares to the unsurpassable greatness of receiving the gifts of God—the forgiveness of sins, life, and salvation? In this Sacrament, Amos's preaching of grace comes to us. There, at the altar, our God promises to "restore the fortunes of My people Israel" and "inhabit" us (9:14). In that sacred meal, the medicine of divine immortality comes to us and we are truly planted in His kingdom, His land—never again to be uprooted (9:15).

Amos's preaching comes to a close in our ears at the Lord's Supper. There the fruits of the Last Day, the fruits of the tree of the cross, come to us. There judgment and mercy meet. There the nations that oppose our God come to an end. There the remnant is restored and joy given freely. And not only Amos but all the prophets, even until John, proclaim the Christ who comes to save us!

Concluding Activities

Conclude the session with an appropriate prayer and announce the next *LifeLight* topic.

Small-Group Leaders Material

The Prophet Amos, by Juan de Borgoña. SuperStock/SuperStock

Getting into the Book of the Twelve

A Survey of the Minor Prophets

Preparing for the Session

Central Focus

The "Minor Prophets" have nothing minor to deliver. What you get in this Book of the Twelve is Christ and Him crucified for Israel, for Judah, and for you!

Objectives

That participants, led by the Holy Spirit working through God's Word, will

1. understand the unique way in which God's Word unfolds by reading the Minor Prophets as one Book of the Twelve;

2. compare the underlying theme of this Book of the Twelve with the theme of Scripture as a whole, as seen on the cross of Christ;

3. find comfort in the sweet Gospel proclamation of the twelve prophets, receiving a new and confident hope in Christ; and

4. apply the Scripture to their own lives, growing in service to the Lord.

For the Small-Group Leader

Small-Group Discussion Helps

Day 1 • Hosea 2:16–23; Amos 5:18–27; Malachi 4

1. a. Answers will vary, based on translation and edition. Participants should recognize that each of the three major prophetic books is roughly the same size, and that the twelve Minor Prophets together are also a similar size.

b. This suggests that perhaps these twelve were intended to be read together and travel together on one scroll.

2. a. Hosea presents a day that is full of great reversals and wonderful blessings.

b. In "that day," the Lord promises to restore the marriage and free His people from bondage to Baal. He promises to make a new covenant with them, bring an end to war and strife, and bestow upon His people righteousness and justice, love and mercy. The earth will produce crops, and the people will be restored to their God.

3. a. Amos presents the same day in completely opposite terms. This day is a day of judgment and condemnation—"darkness," as Amos calls it.

b. The Lord promises to hunt down Israel's sin and destroy it; it cannot hide.

4. Both Hosea and Amos are right. This is what the Day of the Lord is—judgment to the one who keeps his sin to himself, but righteousness and joy to the one whose sin is covered (see Psalm 32). If we read the twelve prophets as entirely separate, we might wonder which is right and which is wrong. But if we take them together, we assume that this day is both judgment and blessing together.

5. Malachi emphasizes this Day of the Lord as a total end—either destruction or blessing. He promises the coming Messiah, "the sun of righteousness," as well as the Elijah who comes before. Major themes will include promises of the coming Christ, Law and Gospel, and a return to Moses and the covenant made at Horeb.

Day 2 • Zephaniah 1:14–16; Joel 1:15; John 19:31–37; Zechariah 12:10–13:1

6. Zephaniah intends a quick repentance. He calls for a fear of what we deserve and a hope that God might not do what He says He will do.

7. a. "The day of the Lord" is sometimes called Judgment Day. It's often spoken of in the New Testament.

b. It is hard to say when the Day of the Lord will be. Most participants should have in mind the second coming of Christ, which we confess in the Creed. On the other hand, and where the following questions lead, it is also the cross, where Jesus cries out, "It is finished" (John 19:30).

8. a. Answers may vary.

b. It is clearly a very fearful thing to have the Lord coming with destruction.

9. Good Friday—the day of Christ's crucifixion. This is the day when all the Scripture find their fulfillment. On that day, reconciliation was made between man and God, and the atonement for sin was made complete.

10. **Challenge question.** Zechariah speaks of this piercing as happening on "that day." This suggests that the crucifixion of Jesus (Good Friday) is the fulfillment of the Day of the Lord.

Day 3 • Haggai 1:1; Obadiah 1; Hosea 1:1; Amos 1:1; Micah 1:1; Haggai 1:1; Zechariah 1:1

11. a. Almost all the superscriptions contain the prophet's name, his father or ancestor's name, that the Word of the Lord came to him, and under what kings this all happened. These superscriptions vary from prophet to prophet, but the same general pattern survives in each.

b. Most notable might be those prophets with hardly any superscription at all (e.g., Obadiah).

12. a. Haggai provides the name of the king and the year, month, and day of the prophecy.

b. Haggai proclaimed this prophecy during August or September 520 B.C.

13. **Challenge question.** Some try dating Obadiah based on similar themes to other prophets (e.g., the words against Edom in Jeremiah). Some see the mention of "exiles of Jerusalem" (Obadiah 20) and locate it with the Babylonian exile. Still others consider where it lies within the Book of the Twelve—after Amos and before Jonah and Micah (all probably written in the eighth century BC). While this deduction isn't certain, these are the clues left to us.

14. a. The three prophets mention Judah kings Uzziah, Jotham, Ahaz, and Hezekiah, and Israel kings Jeroboam and Joash. The fact that there is some overlap suggests that Hosea, Amos, and Micah were active at roughly the same time. Hosea, Amos, and Micah all prophesied in the mid to late eighth century BC.

b. There were approximately two months between the time Haggai prophesied and when Zechariah prophesied. Both were in the late sixth century BC, at least two hundred years after the first minor prophets.

15. Book Three of the Psalter includes psalms by Asaph, the Sons of Korah, David, Heman, and Ethan. Just as the psalms were collected for their common history and content, so the Book of the Twelve may be viewed as a compatible and arranged composition. The twelve Minor Prophets are almost like a mini version of the Bible. They were written over many years, by many hands, in many different settings—and they ultimately point us to God's grace in Christ Jesus.

Day 4 • Luke 24:13–27; Zechariah 9:9–17; 13:7–9

16. Jesus makes clear to the Emmaus disciples (and also to us) that the Old Testament prophets (including, therefore, the Books of Hosea, Joel, and Amos) clearly point to the life, death, and resurrection of the Messiah. That is their main point.

17. This prophecy was fulfilled on Palm Sunday. Just a few days before our Lord would be betrayed and crucified, Jesus rode into Jerusalem (as prophesied by Zechariah) and was greeted with palm branches and loud Hosannas (Matthew 21:1–11).

18. Christ is the shepherd who was pierced (stricken) for us. When this occurred, the sheep scattered—most especially His early disciples. And yet, by this striking of the shepherd, the covenant is restored and the people again have access to their God.

19. *For personal reflection. Sharing optional.* Answers will vary. The participants may, for example, remark that they used to regard the Old Testament as being merely a Jewish book that has little to do with Christians. They may respond that the Old Testament never used to make any sense to them, but now that they know that it points them to Jesus, it is becoming more clear—knowing that it is about Christ means that they know how to read and understand it.

Day 5 • Jonah 3:4–10; Micah 4:6–7; Nahum 3

20. Many might say "Law" because they assume the Old Testament is chiefly Law. Others, having learned that this is all about Christ, might say "Gospel." The reality is that these twelve well balance Law and Gospel—you're going to get both here!

21. In 3:4, Jonah enters Nineveh preaching the Law—the judgment for Nineveh's sin. But Nineveh believes the preaching, calls for drastic measures of repentance, and then delights in the Gospel of God—the forgive-

ness of sin. God first promised destruction, but then does not do it.

22. a. In this particular passage, Micah is not addressing those who are refusing to repent or reveling in their pridefulness—this is not a message of condemnation.

b. Here, Micah is addressing those who have been hurt: the broken, the exiled, the afflicted, and the lonely. For them, Micah preaches the Day of the Lord as pure and sweet Gospel.

23. *For personal reflection. Sharing optional.* Answers will vary. The participants may indicate that such a statement from God would be terrifying (as it should be!) and that it would drive them to repentance. However, some may state that if we were in such a state of persistent unrepentance that God would say such a thing, then we probably would not really care if He were against us.

A Mysterious Love Story

Hosea 1–3

Preparing for the Session

Central Focus

Hosea sets the stage for the Book of the Twelve to be a story of repentance and great reversals, where God ultimately wins us back with His unquenchable and gracious love for us.

Objectives

That participants, led by the Holy Spirit working through God's Word, will

1. recognize that the relationship between Hosea and Gomer is a depiction of God's love for us;

2. interpret the great reversals of Hosea in light of the great reversal that Christ enacts on the cross for us; and

3. come to critique their own lives in terms of repentance and absolution, recognizing the depths to which God descends for them in Christ.

For the Small-Group Leader

Small-Group Discussion Helps

Day 1 • Hosea 1:1–3

1. Jeroboam I had constructed worship sites in the north without the promise or command of God. Jeroboam II had continued this practice, as well as the practice of permitting worship both of the Lord (the God of Israel) and of Baal (the god of the Canaanites). This is the sin of idolatry.

2. a. God commands Hosea to take a wife of ill-repute and have children with her.

b. Hosea does as God commanded.

3. While marriage is a holy institution and something to be held in high regard by everyone, this particular match was not likely to have elevated Hosea in people's minds. A marriage with such a woman as Gomer would have been viewed as scandalous. This marriage would surely discredit Hosea's reputation and probably even his word. He, too, would become an outcast.

4. Even today, with a cultural numbness to promiscuity, a marriage to a harlot would still be unbecoming for one's social reputation. And if it were a pastor in such a union, surely the people would be scandalized. Such a scandal would detract from the pastor's ability to minister to the congregation.

5. *For personal reflection. Sharing optional.* Answers will vary. The question asks for a rather personal response. The participants may prefer not to share their answers.

Day 2 • Hosea 1:4–9

6. The name Jezreel has two major meanings, both brought out in Hosea. The first is the valley of slaughter recorded in 2 Kings 10. To name the child Jezreel is to commemorate the blood spilled in that valley—almost as if God mourned the death of those prophets of Baal. The other meaning of Jezreel, what it actually translates to, is "God sows." This meaning, however, is less implied in Hosea 1:4–5 as it is in the reversal of the name in Hosea 2:21–23.

7. By naming this daughter "No Mercy," God is undoing His own name—both who He is and what He does for His people. Receiving the name "No Mercy" indicates that this child would be a living testimony to God's withdrawing His grace from the Israelites.

8. In the third child, God is undoing His covenant with His people. What makes Israel who they are is that He is their God. This is the judgment, the undoing of God's person and work for Israel.

9. **Challenge question.** For some interpreters, it seemed far too scandalous to think that God would command His prophet such things. However, these passages should not be understood as some kind of allegory or metaphor. It reads like a historical narrative. Hosea was literally commanded by God to do these things—and so, as we read, Hosea did them.

Day 3 • Hosea 1:10–2:1

10. Hosea 1:1–9 is chiefly Law. It is very clearly a condemnation of the people.

11. The word "yet" pulls us up from the darkness of the judgment and into the light of God's grace. Here we suddenly enter into Hosea's preaching of the Gospel. The people would again be God's children.

12. a. These verses present two very different pictures—one of grace and forgiveness and the other of judgment and condemnation.

b. Nevertheless, we can say that both texts are pointing to the same day. For that day would be a day of judgment to those holding onto their sin and a day of joy to those whose sin is covered.

13. The great reversal comes ultimately and only in Christ—first in His work on the cross for us, and then in the giving of His cross to us through the preaching of the Gospel and the giving out of the Lord's gifts in the Sacraments. We, who due to our sins should not be counted as God's people, are forgiven in Christ and are now children of God forever.

14. Israel, the people of God, is the intended audience for Hosea's preaching. However, as we have seen, these prophetic words from God can be applied to us as well.

Day 4 • Hosea 2:2–23

15. This passage is specifically referring to Gomer (and her children) but, as we see in our Ezekiel passage, Gomer in her sins represents sinful Israel.

16. a. God promises to act in wrath on account of Israel's sin.

b. Yet He intends by His wrath only that Israel repent and believe. His wrath is never the intended end, but rather is a means to His grace.

17. a. God's actions are certainly justified.

b. Gomer deserves to be put out from the family—even stoned to death as the Scriptures relate. And even more than Gomer, all of Israel deserves this punishment. Their idolatry ("whoring" after other gods) is no different from Gomer's adultery. Paul tells us in Romans 6:23 that the wages of sin is death.

18. Here, God begins to woo Israel. He will "allure" her, "speak tenderly" to her, and give her gifts. Now we see the gracious working of the great reversal. This is where God reverses who Israel is and who the children are and gives them a new reality. This is where He promises to raise Israel to where she was intended to be.

19. Answers may vary. God longs to have mercy on sinners. In response to all that God promises to do and does for us, we confess who He is, based on His Word. "[We] shall say, 'You are My God.'" That, for instance, is what the Creed teaches: a faithful response to what God has already spoken to us. That is also what our lives declare as we strive to live in ways that are pleasing to God and share the hope of His mercy with others.

Day 5 • Hosea 3

20. Hosea is to disregard Gomer's adultery and take her back. Again, he is to have her as his wife.

21. God loves His people to such a degree that He will not have the marriage covenant broken—the two have become one flesh.

22. The mystery is Christ and the Church—not two, but one flesh. Marriage is a living depiction of the union between Christ, the heavenly Bridegroom, and His Bride, the Church. Therefore, this whole drama revolving around Hosea and Gomer was a living depiction—and prophecy in actions rather than in words—of the promised work of the Savior.

23. *For personal reflection. Sharing optional.* Answers will vary.

Standing Trial

Hosea 4:1–11:11

Preparing for the Session

Central Focus

The God who acts does so in terms of Law and Gospel. He brings us up on charges that we are all guilty of; and then, by the judgment rendered on His Son, sets us free. This we must learn to know over and over and over again!

Objectives

That participants, led by the Holy Spirit working through God's Word, will

1. understand who they are in light of Israel's sins of old;
2. recognize who God is—the One who brings repentance and new life;
3. distinguish between these two understandings, trusting God to do all things well for them; and
4. daily repent from sins of omission and commission, and live actively by faith.

For the Small-Group Leader

Small-Group Discussion Helps

Day 1 • Hosea 4

1. The expression varies depending on which Bible translation one is reading from. The Lord has a "controversy" (ESV) or a "charge" (NIV) against His people because they have no faith or knowledge of God.

2. Answers may vary, but ultimately we would be left defenseless, since all the charges are true! Our only appeal is in Christ, in what He has done for us. That ends all controversy and answers any and all charges that could ever be made against us.

3. **Challenge question.** Answers will vary. It should be noted that although all sins are equally condemned by God, they may affect human life to different degrees.

4. a. Gomer's adultery prophetically depicts the idolatry of Israel. Adultery is really a metaphor for idolatry.

b. The phrase "play the whore" reminds us of Hosea's adulterous and promiscuous wife, Gomer. God cared for His people as a husband cares for his wife (in the New Testament, the Church is called the Bride of Christ), but the people were continually unfaithful to God; they flirted with and joined their hearts to idols instead.

Day 2 • Hosea 4:1–6

5. The biblical idea of knowledge extends far beyond an accumulation of facts. It is relational, or intimate. To know someone could imply a sexual encounter or the intimacy of faith. To know God is to "fear, love, and trust in God above all things" (Luther's Small Catechism).

6. a. Often, we can tell if a person knows God.

b. Language, actions, hobbies, and care are all reflected in a Christian life. Sometimes we get surprised, but in general the faith of the heart forms and bends and guides the character of the body and life.

7. Just as our knowledge of God implies an intimacy of faith and love, so also does God's knowledge of us. He knows us in the way of a marriage covenant—one that He will not break.

8. *For personal reflection. Sharing optional.* Answers will vary.

Day 3 • Hosea 5:1–6:3

9. The priests, the king, the king's officials, and the whole people of Israel are held liable to God's judgment.

10. This is terrible news. At first God says He will rot the people away, and then tear them to pieces, and then bring His judgment so final and complete that "no one shall rescue" (5:14). No message from God could be worse than this.

11. God's place is where He has promised to be: the temple in Jerusalem. That is where the Lord's people must come to meet Him.

12. For us living in this New Testament era, we know that the place where God is for us is in the person of Jesus Christ, our new temple (John 2:19–21). In His death and resurrection, we have all that was distributed from the old temple: forgiveness of sins through the blood of the sacrifice and peace with God.

13. *For personal reflection. Sharing optional.* Answers may vary.

Day 4 • Hosea 6:4–8:14

14. The Lord has used the prophets as His instruments. By them and their words, He has carved away at the sinful nature and purified His people.

15. *For personal reflection. Sharing optional.* Answers will vary. Participants may give answers that include feelings of remorse or contrition and the strong desire for forgiveness. Some may answer that in some instances they felt anger or indignation at having their sins revealed to them—so often, we all prefer to ignore our offenses and pretend they do not exist.

16. In both cases, Jesus is rebuking the Pharisees, who want to trust in their sacrificial work rather than the sacrifice of Christ (the mercy of God). Our own efforts or striving (no matter how perfect) could never make us, who are already sinful, acceptable to God. We can be pleasing to Him only though the full and perfect atonement made by the sacrifice of our Lord Christ.

17. Israel has missed noticing all that God has done for her. It's a bit like buying a bouquet of flowers for your wife and then giving them to your neighbor's wife instead. Israel forgot who her husband is. She did all sorts of great sacrificial work, but all for a non-god, Baal.

18. a. Without God, all the work, sacrifices, and devotion are for naught.

b. Answers may vary.

Day 5 • Hosea 9:1–3; 10:8; 11:1–11

19. In verse 3, Hosea describes a reversal of the exodus as well as the coming Assyrian exile.

20. The full judgment for sins (even for the sin of idolatry) fell on Christ on the cross. Condensed in those three hours on the cross was our Lord's suffering the eternal penalty for all the sins of all the world. Through faith in Him, we are delivered from judgment and will never know that condemnation.

21. a. This passage refers back to the calling out of the Hebrews from Egypt and alludes to the exodus with Moses.

b. The Father cared for His Son by rescuing Him from Herod.

c. Answers may vary but should include personal descriptions of God's kindness.

22. God's character is ultimately that of love. God loves His people in this way, that He turns His wrath away from them and onto His Son at the cross (see John 3:16). He is the God of mercy.

23. **Challenge question.** Answers will vary. By saying that He is not as we are, God is stating that He does not act as we would. He does not treat us as our sins deserve. In fact, He even sacrificed His only-begotten Son to spare us from the condemnation we all deserve so that we would receive infinitely more than we deserve: life eternal.

The Fear of the Lord Is the Beginning of Wisdom

Hosea 11:12–14:9

Preparing for the Session

Central Focus

Hosea ends his introduction to the Book of the Twelve with a call to wisdom. We are truly wise in recognizing who God is and what God has done for us, and in trusting Him to do it again and again!

Objectives

That participants, led by the Holy Spirit working through God's Word, will

1. wrestle with some of the textual difficulties presented in Hosea;
2. apply God's charge against Israel to their own lives;
3. interpret God's dealing with them in light of who He is for them; and
4. hear God's voice to them in the preaching and teaching of their pastors.

For the Small-Group Leader

Small-Group Discussion Helps

Day 1 • Hosea 11:12–12:2

1\. a. According to the ESV translation of the Bible, Judah is presented favorably. This translation renders the Hebrew text as declaring that Judah was still walking with God and faithful to Him.

b. According to the NIV translation of the Bible, Judah is unruly toward God, while God remains faithful. In this understanding of the Hebrew text, Judah is tossed into the same judgment as Ephraim.

2\. a. Here, just two verses after the text we considered in question 1, the Lord indicts Judah for the people's sins.

b. Unless there is a major break in thought between 12:1 and 12:2, the ESV translation would seem incompatible with the broader context. As a consequence, some might prefer the NIV translation, though it might be regarded as smoothing over a difficult reading rather than taking the words as they stand.

3\. Ephraim breaks the covenant with God but pursues a covenant with Assyria and trade with Egypt. Hosea illustrates Israel's self-interest and indifference toward God.

4\. *For personal reflection. Sharing optional.* Answers will vary.

a. Participants may emphasize examples of God's fatherly love toward them.

b. As the Lord loves and mentors us, we may return these kindnesses to others.

Day 2 • Hosea 12:3–6

5\. This allusion refers to the birth of Esau and Jacob (Genesis 25:24–26). They were twins, and Esau was born first, so he was considered the older brother. Jacob was born immediately after Esau, for he had grabbed on to Esau's heel. Therefore, he was named "Jacob": "He that takes by the heel." The expression refers to Jacob's competition with his older and favored brother. It may also refer to the competition between Esau's descendants (Edom) and Jacob's descendants (Israel).

6\. This verse refers back to the account where Jacob is at a ford of the Jabbok. A "man" comes and wrestles with him. At the end of the passage, we learn that this was actually God in the appearance of a man. He wrestled with Jacob and then blessed him. Israel, as Jacob's descendants, should likewise pursue God's blessing.

7\. As Jacob asked and pleaded to know God's name and receive His blessing, so Israel sought Him in prayer.

8\. When Jacob met God, all Israel met God and entered into a bond with Him through the patriarchs.

9\. In making these references to Jacob, God is calling the people of Judah to repent and return to this God who so blessed their ancestor and who has promised to bless them as well. He would have us do the same.

Day 3 • Hosea 12:5–14

10\. The gift of the name is a constant call to repentance: sorrow over sin and faith in God's grace. It is also, therefore, a promise of forgiveness.

11\. a. Israel had wandered from God and His ways and needed Him to find the way back.

b. Returning to the Lord is the same as repenting of sins. Repentance is always a gift of God, never an act of willpower or self-discipline on our part; we do not cause repentance to well up within ourselves. Rather, we are brought to it by the working of the Holy Spirit through the Word of God. His Word of Law brings contrition. His Word of Gospel brings the faith that receives God's forgiveness.

12. a. God is saying He will make Ephraim again dwell in tents; He will return the Northern Kingdom to wandering in the wilderness, as they did under Moses.

b. Since all Christians are also sinners, they need to repent daily, as Jesus teaches in the Lord's Prayer.

13. **Challenge question.** Answers will vary, but all should mention the Office of the Holy Ministry, wherein a called and ordained servant of Christ stands in the stead and by the command of Christ. Therefore, the faithful proclamation the pastor makes to us is not simply his words, but is truly God's Word for us.

14. a. The prophet Moses became the shepherd of the people of Israel during their years of slavery under Pharaoh and through the ten plagues.

b. This service resulted in the marriage covenant between the Lord and His people, Israel.

Day 4 • Hosea 13:1–13

15. The source of their guilt was their reliance on pagan idolatry rather than faith in the Lord. Specifically, they worshiped Baal—and did so "more and more" (v. 2). This involved the making and venerating of metal idols—worshiping the creature rather than the creator—and also engaging in human sacrifice.

16. As we read in Romans 6:23, the wages of sin is always death. Here in Hosea, we see this judgment being given to the people of Ephraim for their idolatry. So they will be like smoke from a window, floating aimlessly away.

17. *For personal reflection. Sharing optional.* Answers will vary, although most will likely agree that sinfulness can increase without us necessarily noticing. Perhaps some will mention the old story about how to boil a frog. If you put a frog in boiling water, it will jump out immediately. However, if you put a frog into a pot of cold water, then increase the temperature gradually, it will stay in the pot, never realizing the danger, until it is boiled. Perhaps we could also liken this to sheep. As they graze, they go about eating and walking and eating and walking, not necessarily paying close attention to where they are going. Then they look up and realize they have strayed from the flock. Likewise, we can very easily go about following our sinful nature and never realize the danger or how far we have strayed until it is too late.

18. Answers will vary. Discussion might turn to abortion. Our society's concern and legal protection for endangered animals contrasts ironically with the lack of concern for the unborn (as seen with the vast number of abortions performed). Are we not "kissing calves" while engaging in human sacrifice? Yet even such sins may be forgiven by the Christ, who humbled Himself to bear our sin and be our only Savior. Urge others to call upon Him when temptation or guilt assails them.

19. a. God likens Himself to a bear that will tear them, a lion that will devour them, and a wild beast that will rip them open. God states that He will take away their king, leave them helpless, and destroy them because of their idolatry.

b. God responds here with another heavy dosage of Law.

Day 5 • Hosea 13:14–14:9

20. Hosea intends 13:14 to be a deep-seated judgment. Paul reverses it for some comforting Gospel promises.

21. Answers will vary. However, yes, Christians may pray for judgment upon the enemies of the faith. The Psalms give us cause to pray such imprecatory prayers from time to time (see Psalms 35, 59, 69, 79, 109, 137, 140). Ultimately, our enemy against whom we pray is the unholy trinity: the world, our sinful flesh, and the devil.

22. Hosea directs the people to return to the Lord with "words." By this, he means that the people are to come back (return/repent) to God with God's words. The people were to speak to God what God had first said to them. This is always the way for us. God speaks and we listen, then we confess His Word of truth back to Him. This is the basis of our worship and our repentance. We receive His Word in the Scriptures; through that Word, the Holy Spirit forms and directs our hearts to God.

23. The Lord will heal, love, give growth, and protect His people. His anger will turn away from them. Rather than being their destruction, God will be their life and their rest.

24. a. The Lord speaks to Ephraim, that is, the northern tribes of Israel.

b. Certainly, Hosea intends the first readers and hearers to remain in both the faith and love of God. However, these words intentionally also speak beyond them to us.

Judgment: Despair or Hope?
Joel 1:1–2:11

Preparing for the Session

Central Focus

The judgment described in the first half of Joel is a plague/word/cross that appears in each and every life. As this Word is executed, those who cling to their sin find only despair; but for those who receive the work of this cross in faith, there is only hope—leading to life everlasting.

Objectives

That participants, led by the Holy Spirit working through God's Word, will

1. understand the complexity of Scripture in general and the unique witness of Joel in particular;
2. compare the suffering of the locust invasion to the various crosses they bear today;
3. interpret the prophetic Last Day in full view of the crucifixion of Christ the Lord; and
4. live for the Lord, anticipating His return.

For the Small-Group Leader

Small-Group Discussion Helps

Day 1 • Joel 1:1–12

1. All we know about Joel from this verse is that he is the son of Pethuel and that he is a prophet—the Word of the Lord came to him.

2. a. There are actually two possible meanings of those statements. Joel could either be speaking of what has come previously or of what is to come, the terrible destruction of the locusts he describes in his prophecy.

b. They have no history of such a devastating attack.

3. The point here is a total destruction. As if one wave of locusts wouldn't be bad enough, each would be followed by yet another wave of devastation. If anything was left, the next would consume it, and so forth.

4. For an agrarian society, the destruction of crops means the downfall of commerce, food, health, and the entire sacrificial system. All aspects of life suffer from this destruction, which may bring famine.

5. a. The commands are to awake, lament, and be ashamed.

b. Each seems to be in progression from one to the next. Awake: notice the destruction. Lament: recognize your pain from this destruction. Be ashamed: realize that this is a judgment on you because of your guilt.

Day 2 • Joel 1:4–12

6. Those hearing Joel should fear that they had become like Egypt of old. The same plague that ravaged the pagan Egyptians was now falling on them because of their sins. They would know that they could face total destruction because of their sins, as did Pharaoh.

7. All references to the total destruction of locusts point us toward the final Judgment Day to come. Exodus anticipates Joel, and Joel anticipates Christ's victory over sin, death, and the devil on the cross. Revelation depicts the reality of the cross through an apocalyptic vision. Note in that vision that those marked with the seal of God (i.e., marked as being God's own) are preserved from harm. The plague in Revelation falls only on the unbelievers—for the believers, all judgment has already fallen on Christ.

8. As Isaiah speaks of the vine as Israel facing God's judgment, we can view this destruction of the land in Joel as ultimately a destruction of Israel for its sins.

9. We can think of the destruction of Israel in light of the crucifixion of Jesus, the true Son of God. On the cross, Christ, the true vine, was destroyed. However, Jesus also speaks of the pruning of branches, referring to the challenges and afflictions we experience, through which God prepares us to grow abundant fruit.

10. The drink and grain offering accompanied the regular visitation and gracious presence of the Lord. Without these, the people would no longer have a gracious meeting with their God. So we can see that their sins have resulted not just in the devastation of their earthly goods but also in a separation between them and God.

Day 3 • Joel 1:13–16

11. These are very often noted in the Old Testament as outward signs of repentance.

12. Joel does not specifically state what their transgressions were. They may be guilty of being persistently unrepentant in their idolatry.

13. Both days are prepared by and come from God. However, Joel's Day of the Lord is very bad news, expressing God's wrath for breaking His Law. Hosea's description emphasizes God's grace and restoration for His people.

14. a. In our sin, the Lord's presence terrifies us (consider Adam and Eve before and after their sin). His presence is not always pleasant: if He is there with wrath, we cannot stand.

b. But if He is there with grace, we are lifted from our graves. As the Lord declares us righteous through faith, we long for His presence, even when we fall.

c. Answers may vary.

Day 4 • Joel 1:17–2:3

15. When our crosses seem heavy—even when, in truth, they were self-inflicted—we can easily start to wonder whether God is really good, whether He is good to us, or whether He really does want us to be well.

16. Joel turns from addressing the people to addressing the Lord. Here, the prophet prays for the people, that the Lord would not abandon His people or punish them forever but that He would have compassion for them and deliver them.

17. With this reference to a trumpet blast, Joel hopes to awaken (1:5) the people to recognize their sin and, consequently, to repent of it.

18. Joel depicted the punishment for the people's sin as a land like Eden being devoured by fire and turned into a wasteland. We can remember that Eden was lost to us and turned into a locked fortress that we may not enter as a result of the sin of our first parents in disobeying the Lord's command.

Day 5 • Joel 2:4–11

19. Fear takes the color from our faces. Recognizing what we truly deserve from God on account of our sin should cause us great fear and horror.

20. a. The invading locusts/armies are described in human terms, as using war horses, chariots, and fire. They use tactics such as charging, marching, and scaling the walls.

b. Historically, the most devastating armies to enter Israel were the Assyrians in the eighth century BC and the Babylonians in the sixth century BC. Prior to the eighth century BC, there were various raids and attacks by the Edomites and others.

21. It is the voice of the Lord that terrifies both the heavens and the earth. God speaks in His wrath the accusations and threats of the Law such that all of creation trembles.

22. The army is God's army: His voice, His army, His locusts, His Assyrians (or whomever). This army has been raised up and sent by God. It is His instrument performing His work of judgment.

23. **Challenge question.** None of us could ever hope to withstand God's judgment, for we are all fallen and sinful. Nevertheless, there is One who has withstood, for He is perfectly righteous. As our Lord Christ died, forsaken by God for our sins, and then rose again triumphant on the third day, He gave us the certainty to know that we, though burdened by our sins, will not be destroyed in the judgment but will be sustained and will rise again on the Last Day. Then we will share in glory of Christ's perfect righteousness forever.

God for Us

Joel 2:12–3:21

Preparing for the Session

Central Focus

When everything in life seems hopeless, when all seems lost, when the time is up and the end is near—there's always Christ for you!

Objectives

That participants, led by the Holy Spirit working through God's Word, will

1. delight in the literary transition from death to life that Joel provides;

2. apply the moment of salvation provided for Israel to themselves;

3. come to defend the many ways in which God is gracious to His people of all times, even in the Old Testament; and

4. live by the Spirit each day.

For the Small-Group Leader

Small-Group Discussion Helps

Day 1 • Joel 2:12–17

1. God asks the people to return to Him in repentant faith and love.

2. The Lord founds their repentance on who He is: gracious, merciful, slow to anger, and abounding in steadfast love. And so it is for us as well. We do not rest our faith in the quality or depth of our repentance, but rather in the character of God: merciful, forgiving, and gracious.

3. Answers will vary. God's judgment shows that situations can reach a point of no return with Him. However, the Scripture constantly emphasizes the patience and mercy of God as well as His ability and willingness to forgive all sins. To these truths we cling when our hearts condemn us or when we fear for others who do not repent.

4. Joel doesn't seek only an outward display but the inward change of a broken spirit and a contrite heart. A mere outward display is simply self-righteousness, but the inward change of heart is a reliance on the righteousness of Christ.

5. **Challenge question.** Answers will vary. The matter of God's repentance raises issues for the theologians who would emphasize God's attributes of unchangeableness and foreknowledge. The translation "relent" softens the blow, since "repent" might mistakenly lead people to conclude that God sins—certainly the wrong conclusion. Ultimately, this is a mystery of God's nature. Trust His Word with an undivided heart and don't worry about the rest.

Day 2 • Joel 2:15–17

6. Joel calls for a public act of repentance.

7. The clergy (priests and court prophets) lead the prayers and worship of communal repentance. They select psalms of communal repentance. They consecrate the people.

8. Even the youngest children must attend. Bridegrooms, normally exempt from even military duty, must leave the wedding chambers with their brides!

9. As our High Priest, Jesus intercedes for us and leads us to intercede for ourselves and others.

10. Jesus' intercession, in divine wisdom, is perfect and complements His perfect and redeeming sacrifice, which cleanses us from all sin. Even the best human ministers cannot match this. Nevertheless, we praise God that our pastor, who stands in the stead and by the command of Christ, intercedes on our behalf before God. He prays for us (and with us). At the same time, he is also the mouthpiece of God for us. It works two ways.

Day 3 • Joel 2:18–27

11. The Lord hears and responds with full grace and restoration.

12. a. The attacker comes from the north.

b. Mesopotamian armies invaded Israel from the north, crossing the fords of the Euphrates River. The Assyrians and Babylonians also came from the northern direction.

13. The early rain and the latter rain will refresh the land and restore the crops the people lost.

14. The Lord promises renewed crops and land, the removal of the enemy and oppression, joy and gladness, rain and fruitfulness.

15. This is a great reversal, which culminates in the gracious presence of God with His people.

Day 4 • Joel 2:28–32

16. We do not need to fear God's wrath and judgment, for the Lord has done great and marvelous things in sending Christ to redeem us from our sins. The removal of sin by Christ's Word of promise creates the joy and gladness within us that Joel speaks of.

17. Peter preaches from this text to the crowd on the Day of Pentecost (Acts 2), and we find that the words of this prophecy were fulfilled on that day. With the miraculous coming of the Holy Spirit to the apostles and the thousands coming to faith through their preaching and baptizing, Joel's prophecy finds its fulfillment in the temple courts.

18. **Challenge question.** The Holy Spirit continues to come among us whenever and wherever the Word of God is proclaimed in its truth and purity. The Holy Spirit also comes to us through the sacraments—that is, the Word of God with the visible elements of water (Baptism) and bread and wine (the Lord's Supper).

19. This is not a formula or magic spell. Rather, it is a trust and invocation of the God who acts for us with and by His name. To call upon His name is to turn to the Lord in faith and trust in Him for deliverance.

20. The people are waiting for the Day of the Lord; there are frequent appearances of future terms like "will" and "shall" that show this. There is a very clear sense in Joel of a future fulfillment.

Day 5 • Joel 3

21. God condemns the nations for having first scattered the people from their land. Then they treated them as objects for control. Remember that in the Old Testament, the Land of Canaan was frequently referred to as Israel's "inheritance" from God. The land then was a foreshadowing of the eternal inheritance to come on the Last Day when those resurrected to glory will inhabit the new heavens and the new earth. Tearing the Old Testament people away from the land was not just dispossessing the people of their property inheritance, but also falsely declaring that they had no eternal inheritance.

22. For those reading the Book of Joel (presumably those with faith), this condemnation is pure Gospel, as are all the oracles against the nations. The enemies of God will not be successful, but their plans will fail and their deeds will not go unpunished. All of God's people who had been wrongfully abused will be fully vindicated by the Lord Himself.

23. For as long as this present world stands, the Church of Christ will engage in a spiritual battle against authorities and cosmic powers (Ephesians 6:12) that seek to tear us away from Christ. However, we know that no matter how fierce the struggle, our Lord Christ has built His Church, and not even the gates of hell will prevail against it (Matthew 16:18).

24. Our weapon is not the sword or spear, but the Word of God—His commandments and promises. To fight in this battle is to cling to this Word and speak it to each as he or she has need.

25. Our Lord promises to be a stronghold and a refuge for His people. He promises they will be secure and will enjoy the bounty of the new creation to come on the Last Day. Also, God promises that our enemies will be destroyed—no matter how strong they may be. They will never harm us or threaten us again. In Christ, our New Temple, we will be preserved. He truly is our eternal refuge.

From the Nations to Israel—Judgment for All!

Amos 1–2

Preparing for the Session

Central Focus

When the Lord speaks, He speaks to all. None is left out from judgment or blessing. This Word that comes to all mankind is the roar of the Lion of Judah—most loudly and clearly heard in the whispers that came from the cross of Christ.

Objectives

That participants, led by the Holy Spirit working through God's Word, will

1. become familiar with who Amos was and the context in which he preached;

2. associate the word of Amos with the Law/Gospel proclamation of Christ; and

3. discern the all-inclusive character of God's actions toward mankind, reflecting on what that means for each of them in their Christian life.

For the Small-Group Leader

Small-Group Discussion Helps

Day 1 • Amos 1:1

1. The prophets Hosea and Micah were both contemporaries of Amos—they were all serving as prophets of the Lord at about the same time.

2. Amos gives us the time frame of his service as a prophet by making reference to an earthquake.

3. Answers will vary. Allow people to share, but be prepared to move them back to the discussion of biblical names.

4. It could mean that what Amos proclaims is a weighty word—a true burden. This is an accurate description of His prophecies: cutting Law and deeply undeserved Gospel. This name could also mean he himself was a burden (see ch. 7!).

5. The name Jesus means "the Lord saves." This name is fulfilled in the person and work of Jesus, ultimately at the cross and the resurrection. Simply by using His name in faith, we are confessing who He is and what He accomplished for us—that He is God who became man and sacrificed Himself for our sins and rose again for our justification.

Day 2 • Amos 1:1–2

6. a. The Lord is likened to a lion who roars from Zion.

b. Amos will proclaim the Lord's judgment most severely.

7. The Lord and His people are divided from one another due to the people's sin. Lions roar when they seek to intimidate their prey. What could ever be more intimidating than the roar of God? The Lord roars with His voice of judgment to draw His people from their sins and a certain condemnation into repentance and everlasting life.

8. Deep humility is the response of both the pastures and the mountains. All of creation recognizes the voice of the Lord.

9. a. Amos addresses Israel especially.

b. It is important to note that the Lord roars from Zion, from Jerusalem (i.e., from the temple).

c. It was from the temple that God in the Old Testament delivered His grace to His people. For God to be roaring from the temple means that the purpose of this roar is not to destroy us or leave us in despair, but to drive us to repentance and a reliance on Christ as the only One who can deliver us.

Day 3 • Amos 1:3–15

10. a. The sin of Damascus is their threshing of Gilead, a city of the Northern Kingdom.

b. This threshing could be a metaphorical statement of the violence they wreaked against this city of our Lord's Promised Land, or it could be a literal threshing of the land—which might suggest that they treated it as if it were their land and not our Lord's.

11. a. Both Gaza and Tyre, coastal cities of Philistia and Phoenecia, are reprimanded for the sin of exiling our Lord's people.

b. They rooted out a "whole people" that was not theirs to root out. This shows that our Lord desires mercy, even in the midst of judgment.

12. a. Edom had no mercy. Unlike Esau of old (after whom Edom is named), who pitied Jacob in Genesis 33, Edom has pursued his brother Israel and cut him down.

b. This shows that our Lord desires mercy and compassion—and most notably, that He will not keep His wrath forever.

13. a. Like Damascus before, the Ammonites have considered the land of Gilead their own land. To do so, they forcefully destroyed the weakest among them: the women and children.

b. Our Lord denounces this desecration of life—even life in the womb!

Day 4 • Amos 2:1–3

14. a. Moab appears to have exceeded the justice leveled against Edom and acted out of personal anger and hostility.

b. The Lord is bothered most, it seems, because justice is His, as is wrath—Moab was not given to desecrate the bones of the already slain king.

15. This shows that God is the God of the whole world—not just Israel. He is Lord over all of creation—even over the Gentile nations—and He demands from them justice and peace as well.

16. a. These words can be seen as both Law and Gospel.

b. The oracles against the nations are words of strict Law to the nations under judgment, but sweet Gospel to Israel (for whom the words are directed). The promised destruction of God's enemies is a tremendous blessing to God's people.

17. a. Answers may vary, but hopefully participants notice at least these: "For three transgressions of . . . and for four, I will not revoke the punishment"; and "So I will send a fire upon . . ."

b. Participants may notice the numerical associations; for example, 3 transgressions + 4 transgressions = 7 transgressions, with 7 being a number often used in the Bible as symbolizing "completeness." This could then signify that they have committed a complete sin (in some sense), meriting a complete destruction. However, we can also note that 3 + 4 has an accumulating effect (three and then four . . . and then perhaps even more—won't it ever end!), where the sense is "for their continuous sin."

Day 5 • Amos 2:4–16

18. The oracles against the various unbelieving, gentile nations have finished. Now Amos turns these oracles against Judah and Israel—the people of God.

19. Israel in particular appears to be receiving the worst punishment of all the various nations—even worse than the most vicious heathen nation. They certainly have the longest indictment against them. We can only tremble to think of the severity of their punishment. Though they are spared (at least for now) the fire promised to all the others, they are to be set in their place—presumably by this Word of the Lord.

20. a. Answers will vary.

b. Since Christians are still sinful, they continue to need the rebuke of the Law.

21. *For personal reflection. Sharing optional.* Answers will vary. Daily repentance and prayer are the ongoing need of believers, who should flee to Zion rather than hide from God's roar.

22. The participants' answers may include Judgment Day or the destruction of the Kingdoms of Israel and Judah. While those answers are certainly true, we may also recall that God's vengeance on sin is not for anyone—not even the repentant. The punishment is not revoked, but is charged entirely to the Son of God Himself, Jesus Christ. Therefore, we see this punishment being carried out in full on Christ at Golgotha.

The Lord and His People

Amos 3–6

Preparing for the Session

Central Focus

The Lord and His people are not "in a relationship," as social networks might phrase it today. As Hosea taught us, they are married—joined together by the blood of the Lamb. This covenantal union is repeatedly broken by the people of God; yet, it is also repeatedly restored by God Himself through His Word as revealed by the prophet.

Objectives

That participants, led by the Holy Spirit working through God's Word, will

1. critique Israel's unfaithfulness with their own repentant hearts;

2. understand the workings of a prophet in view of the heavenly council; and

3. analyze the name of God in light of His promised presence in and with that name, even among them in their baptismal grace.

For the Small-Group Leader

Small-Group Discussion Helps

Day 1 • Amos 3:1–6

1. a. Each of these rhetorical questions implies the answer "no."

b. They will feel themselves to be God's prey upon whom His trap of the Law has sprung.

2. When we had the metaphor of God as a lion in 1:2, God was roaring at His people. If God is also the lion here in Amos 3, then His people are His prey, caught between His paws—this is a rather fearful depiction.

3. Although it may be disturbing or distressing for us to comprehend, verse 6 certainly implies that the Lord brings about the disaster to the city.

4. They require agreement.

5. Answers will vary. Participants should note that what is most important is that we are walking together with God. Any agreement or unity with others apart from agreement and unity with God may actually be harmful, for we have separated ourselves from God to join with others.

a. Family isn't just a blood or legal bond. It requires real agreement about life and how persons within the family will relate to one another.

b. A congregation's unity depends upon a shared confession, goals, and agreement about how to act in view of these.

c. Similar blessings must prevail for the sake of interchurch relations. Agreeing to disagree may only cover up future conflicts that will emerge later.

Day 2 • Amos 3:7–15

6. The Lord always reveals His Word (will, plan, counsel) to His prophets before He acts upon that Word.

7. a. The prophets are properly forth-tellers.

b. As forth-tellers, the prophets stand in the council of the Lord, hear His Word, and then speak forth that Word. They don't look into the future or predict the future; they simply report what they see—whether it be past, present, or future.

8. The Word revealed to Amos is Law—judgment upon the strongholds in Ashdod and Egypt. However, there is a glimmer of hope for Israel—like two legs pulled from the mouth of a lion, or an ear not totally devoured.

9. The first and most heinous of Israel's sins is the idolatrous practice of Baal worship at the altars of Bethel. The second, which flows from a lack of fear, love, and trust in God above all things, is their idolatry of wealth and riches.

Day 3 • Amos 4

10. This is an example of sarcasm (and a rather biting sarcasm at that, especially for those who had been going to Bethel and Gilgal). Obviously, God does not want anyone to go to the pagan shrines at Bethel and Gilgal and deliberately sin. He doesn't want anyone to transgress His Law or sacrifice to pagan gods.

11. The five afflictions that God placed on His people to lead them to repentance were (1) famine, (2) drought, (3) blight and mildew, (4) pestilence and war, and (5) divine assault. Nevertheless, the people ignored His call and remained obstinate in their idolatry.

12. Israel was certain to meet God in His wrath and vengeance. However, those who repent and turn to Him in faith may face their Maker in peace.

13. These are both hymns. They interrupt the flow of the preaching to herald God as creator and almighty.

14. a. The Lord must remind them and us who He is as often as He can because we forget so easily.

b. When we forget, we fall into the trap of making God how we think He ought to be. We are often tempted to a form of self-idolatry: creating a god in our own image, after our own likeness. How often do we naturally assume that our desires are right and proper—and therefore God-pleasing—without ever really giving any thought to God's commandments? Perhaps, like the Israelites, we need to be reminded of who God really is.

Day 4 • Amos 5:1–13

15. a. Lamentations are common in the Psalms as well as in some of the Prophets. They serve the purpose of changing God's heart or mind by appealing to His mercy.

b. Through his pleas for pity, compassion, and, ultimately, a change of mind, the prophet hopes to get God to "repent" and deliver His people from their suffering.

16. This is really an amazing passage. It truly demonstrates the depth of God's love and concern for us. In this text, God all but begs the people to turn their lustful eyes from idolatry to Him. He pleads with the people, ultimately, to live!

17. When people are called to seek the Lord, they are not to search their hearts or look inside themselves. They are to go back to Jerusalem—the temple in the Old Testament; the church for us New Testament believers—that's where God has promised to be for them and where He distributes His Word and blessings to them.

18. Seeking God is the same as seeking the good. God is good, and a rightly placed faith results in a rightly ordered life and a right regard for one's neighbor.

19. Answers will vary, but they should be directed toward the places where God has promised to be: in His Word and Sacraments. God is in Christ, reconciling the world to Himself through the preaching of the Gospel and through baptizing and communing.

Day 5 • Amos 5:16–6:14

20. Again, God's presence in their midst is not a good thing because His presence here is not a gracious presence. Rather, He is coming in judgment.

21. They will have the Day of the Lord as darkness, divine persecution, hopelessness, and the wrath of God. They will be torn from the Promised Land and sent into exile beyond Damascus.

22. God first despises their feasts because the people make them feasts shared between the Lord and Baal. But He also hates their assemblies because they think that just doing the right outward acts will appease God's wrath. The Lord is not principally concerned with the outward performance of works, but with the faith in the people's hearts.

23. Amos highlights the sins of idolatry, both of Baal and also of their wealth and status. He condemns their lack of hearing the Word and of believing the call to repentance. Certainly, the apathy to the Word and a veneration of wealth and status have a comfortable home among us today. We also increasingly see the true religion mixed in with false religious teachings.

24. a. The opposite of pride is humility and repentance; it is the forsaking of one's self for a full trust in Christ.

b. Clearly, the Israelites should have suppressed their pridefulness and heard God's call to repentance.

The Prophetic Vision

Amos 7–9

Preparing for the Session

Central Focus

The true prophet stands before the face of God, sees and hears the Word God desires to impart, and then goes forth to speak this Word boldly to the Lord's own people. He speaks and does nothing of his own power or strength, but only that which comes from the Lord. And the true prophet delivers nothing else than Christ and Him crucified for us and for all!

Objectives

That participants, led by the Holy Spirit working through God's Word, will

1. comprehend the substance and structure of prophetic vision;
2. rejoice in prophetic intercession, especially the ever-present intercession of Christ on their behalf;
3. discern the fulfillment of all true prophets in the person and work of Jesus Christ; and
4. intercede in prayer for others.

For the Small-Group Leader

Small-Group Discussion Helps

Day 1 • Amos 7:1

1. Answers may vary. Allow some discussion but be prepared to direct the group on to the next question.

2. There is a big difference between society's visions for a preferred future and the scriptural account of prophetic vision. The prophetic vision is the prophet standing in the council of God, seeing what God shows and hearing what God speaks. Society's various visions are grounded in man's desires for the future.

3. Genuine visions (in Scripture) always come from the Lord. If there are no visions, that is not the fault of someone having lost the ability to see them, but it is the Lord who has not given visions.

4. What Amos sees is actually a physical reality. It is not like our dreams or personal aspirations. This is more like standing before God and having Him speak into reality an event before one's eyes.

Day 2 • Amos 7:2–6

5. Amos's first instinct is to pray that God will not do what He said He would do. He prays for Israel's forgiveness and for God to relent from laying this punishment on them.

6. The Lord listens to Amos, repents of the vision, and declares the promise "it shall not be."

7. a. The prophet is given to intercede for the people. Amos pleads for the people because that is his function as prophet—to speak to the people the Word of the Lord and also to speak to the Lord on behalf of the people.

b. God listens because the prophet, even in intercession, is speaking God's Word back to Him.

8. **Challenge question.** Answers may vary, but surely the prophetic intercession ought to encourage our faith that God hears and listens to our prayer.

9. Even today, the continual work of Christ is as our advocate, or intercessor.

Day 3 • Amos 7:7–17

10. It seems there is no intercession because Amos can see that God's word of punishment is now final and complete. Also, as verse 10 shows, Amos is interrupted by Amaziah.

11. a. Amaziah was a priest.

b. The high place of Bethel.

c. He had been set there by the king, not by God. In other words, he was playing church.

12. When the Law comes, as it does from the lips of Amos, three typical responses are to (1) fight the accusations, or make some sort of excuse or self-justification; (2) flee the accusations and deny them either publicly or to yourself; and (3) admit the accusation is true, repent, and believe that the same God who accuses you is the God who is also for you. Amaziah fights by prohibiting Amos's preaching.

13. Amos stands in the stead and by the command of the Lord. It is not his own word he speaks, but the Lord's.

14. The same is true for your pastor. In his preaching, teaching, and leading the church in worship, the pastor proclaims God's words and promises to you.

Day 4 • Amos 8

15. The summer fruit are the last to be harvested. And if they are in the basket, that means the harvest has come, the season is over, the end is near.

16. Silence is not the last word. Even when Jesus breathed His last, the silence was broken on the third day. Trumpets, angels, and finally the Lord's "Peace be with you"—all of these herald the end of silence and the joy of the Lord. God does not delight in judgment, so He brings it to an end in His Son, Jesus.

17. Answers may vary, but the point is that the people of Israel are so disinclined toward the Lord's giving of His gifts that they watch their watches (so to speak), wondering how quickly they can leave and get back to the market to buy, sell, and cheat.

18. a. The worst judgment any of us or them could ever encounter is a removal of the Word (8:11).

b. Answers will vary, but without the Word there can be no forgiveness, no grace, no mercy, no love, no goodness, no rest, and no God. It is only with the Word that we are given and sustained in the faith in Christ and that we receive all the blessings He won for us on the cross: forgiveness of sins, life, and salvation.

Day 5 • Amos 9

19. The vision is of the destruction of the high places in Israel.

20. A sudden change occurs from verse 10 to 11. The prophet turns from proclaiming Law to proclaiming Gospel: the day of darkness turns to light; death gives way to life. This helps us see that the total prophecy was not about pronouncing judgment but urging repentance.

21. a. Jesus fulfills the booth of David by being Himself the true Son of David (see Matthew 1:1).

b. The raising up of this booth is seen on Easter Sunday, where the Christ is raised from the dead.

22. In Amos, as in the Book of the Twelve as a whole, the Day of the Lord is a day of both Law and Gospel—Law to those who would rather keep their sin and not heed our Lord's call to repentance, but Gospel to those who despair of themselves and come as beggars, hoping that perhaps God will yet turn and be merciful.